Understanding
The Book Of Job

"Separating What Is True From
What Is Truth"

by
Tom Tompkins

WINLIGHT MINISTRIES

Unless noted, all scriptures are taken from
the King James Version of the Bible.

Contents

Preface

It is safe to say at the very least, that the Bible is a fascinating book. A book full of many true tales, even struggles and disappointments, along with much information intended to help people grow and mature in their relationship with God. After all, it is impossible to have a positive relationship with someone we have not gotten to know and this principal applies to all relationships including one with God.

While there is more than one way that our Heavenly Father reveals Himself to us, reading the Bible is one of the most important methods by which we can get to know Him. However, many shy away from reading the Old Testament for various reasons and one reason high on most people's list is due to the "gloom and doom". However, not reading the Old Testament portion of the Bible is similar to using half of the pieces to a 1000 piece puzzle. We will never see the big picture if we only use half of the included pieces.

One of the most **misunderstood** and **misused** books of the Bible is the book of Job. Yes, the book of Job is filled with suffering and difficult times in the life of Job and his family and friends. In turn, the book of Job has become a favorite among many when it comes to dealing with difficult times in their own life or the lives of others. This particular take, on the book of Job however, is written to help us understand the lessons than can be learned from Job's life. Through it, we can gain a better understanding of the character and nature of God Himself, by looking at the oldest book in the Bible, from a different angle. When we do so, we "change the lens" so-to-speak that we view this incredible story through, and I believe we will see things we otherwise never would have seen.

Chapter 1

Changing Our Viewpoint

Many years ago, I found myself between jobs. At the time, I needed a newer and more reliable vehicle. In turn, I went searching for a job. At this point in time I was in college so I dropped by the student services office to have a look at the job board. I poured over the job board until something caught my eye; car inspector. I wasn't sure what the job involved but since I'm a car person, I became highly interested. I went into the student services office to get more details.

It turned out that this job involved looking over several different makes and models of cars and trucks in order to find transportation related damage. For the most part these vehicles came directly from assembly plants all over the United States. They were all shipped via rail car and had many opportunities to incur damage between the final assembly line inspection and their arrival at the yard where I was working.

My job was to look each vehicle over and find any damage. This included dents, dings, scratches, and scuffs. I carried a hand held computer along with a card on which was listed many codes for many different types of damage. When I found a dent, I would enter the proper code into the hand held computer and repeat the process for any other damage I may have seen. However, there was a very important key to ensuring I did not miss any damage.

That key step was looking at the vehicle from more than just one angle. Depending on how the sun was shining, some defects and damage could be hidden from view if I only stood at the front of the vehicle for my inspection. I was often amazed at what I could see on the driver's door if I simply moved from the front of the vehicle to the rear and changed my perspective.

The book of Job reminds me a lot of our experiences with people. Let's look at "church" as an example.

When we go to church, most people seem to have it all together but we are only seeing what is on the surface level in most cases. I'll use my parents as an example, with their permission of course.

Many years ago, my parents had a rough marriage. Thankfully, things have improved greatly since then, but at this particular point in time, our home was full of strife. However, many people would have never believed this based on what they saw when my parents went to church.

My Dad did not attend church on a regular basis during this period. Nevertheless, when he did attend, everyone was glad to see him. He knew how to make them laugh and had many funny stories to tell. If you saw him and my mom together, it seemed as if they had a great marriage. However, if the members of the church had followed our family home they would have seen a far different picture: the truth!

What was the difference between the viewpoint from church and home? The answer is quite simple: what was seen at church only offered an "on the surface" viewpoint. What took place behind closed doors was the same thing as what takes place beneath the surface.

The book of Job is similar. If we only read the book of Job on an "above the surface" level, it is easy to conclude that God was ultimately the one at the source of Job's struggles.

However, a look much deeper into the book of Job, beneath the surface, reveals a far different picture.

One of the most common problems seen in the Body of Christ today is reading the Bible. Many believers tend to do one of two things. Either they steer clear of the Old Testament all together or they mix the Old Testament with the New Testament. Both processes will create much confusion and inaccurate doctrine. Why, you may ask?

Luke 5:36-39, "Then Jesus gave them this illustration: "No one tears a piece of cloth from a new garment and uses it to patch an old garment. For then the new garment would be ruined, and the new patch wouldn't even match the old garment. 37 And no one puts new wine into old wineskins. For the new wine would burst the wineskins, spilling the wine and ruining the skins. 38 New wine must be stored in new wineskins. 39 But no one who drinks the old wine seems to want the new wine. 'The old is just fine,' they say." NLT

In the parable spoken by Jesus in Luke chapter 5, he was speaking of separating the old from the new. In our case, this applies in the form of separating the Old Testament from the New Testament. The reason is simple. God's way of dealing with man was direct and carried the deserved consequences in the Old Testament and under the Old Covenant. The Old Testament was prior to Jesus coming to the Earth and most certainly prior to his payment for all sin **(1 John 2:2)**. Many still find themselves trying to pour the "old wine" in the modern church by the act of focusing on sin and the punishment for those sins if we don't "get right with God".

It is important that we understand that Jesus paid for all sin one time and one time only as a sacrifice on our behalf.

Obviously, we know that God does not change **(Hebrews 13:8)**, yet God is not judging the sin in our day and age. How can this be? It's very simple. God judged sin once and for all when He sent His Son, Jesus Christ, to hang on the cross in our place **(2 Corinthians 5:21)**. Sin had to be judged and it was, when Jesus took our place as the sacrifice. When we properly understand that sin was dealt with when Jesus went to the cross, it should help us to have a better understanding of the Old Testament. You see, the Old Testament is full of what are known as types and shadows which are different events and prophecies, which point to the much better deal, which is the New Covenant. Yet many today still believe that any natural disaster or other event in which people suffer or lose their lives must be the judgment of God.

We are surely warned of events such as Earthquakes, wars, and rumors of war among many other events during the final days leading up to Jesus' return. However, none of these events are said to be the judgment of God but rather *groanings* from the Earth. If we were truly seeing the judgment and wrath of God being poured out we would hear of the events mentioned in **Revelation 6:16**

"And said to the mountains and rocks, Fall on us, and hide us from the face of him that sitteth on the throne, and from the wrath of the Lamb".

Not a single person is crying out to the rocks or the mountains to fall on them in order to hide from the wrath of God. One conclusion we can draw from **Revelation 6:16** is that God's wrath is far worse than any event we are seeing today.

Yes, we see God judging man in the Old Testament and under the Old Covenant. However, under the New Covenant, God is dealing with man based upon Jesus' completed work on the cross. There are some very fascinating stories in the Old Testament which are meant to help us gain a proper understanding of why Christ had to come to the Earth, be crucified, and rise from the dead. We also need to understand properly what Christ's death, burial, and resurrection have done for us. In changing our viewpoint we need to be able to know the history of a given subject or topic.

In order for us to understand how we are able to live outside of God's judgment and wrath today, we must first understand what brought us to this point today. Studying the Old Testament is meant to accomplish this for us. We can liken the differences between the Old Testament and the New Testament to a marriage or even long-term friendship. When we are really close to a person, we are going to know many details about that person's life. We will know of a wide range of past experiences they have had. We will know about their family and upbringing, schools they have attended, sports they may have played, and so on. We will know about the good and the bad as to their life experiences. In essence, we will be able to look at our knowledge of those many events and understand why that person, with a specific personality and traits to go along with it, is standing before us today. In other words, we need to get to know a person before we can understand why they may act and react in certain ways to certain situations. Knowing about their past is the only way to understand why they are who they are today.

The Bible works in the same manner. We must understand the past in order to be able to grasp the present with a healthy perspective.

Chapter 2

Separating What is True from What is Truth

---W---

"And said, Naked came I out of my mother's womb, and naked shall I return thither: The LORD gave and the LORD has taken away: blessed be the name of the LORD." **Job 1:21**

This is a verse commonly used during funerals and other difficult times throughout life.

If we read **Job 1:21** from a surface level we will automatically assume that Job made an accurate statement. However, upon reading the entire book of Job we are unable to find a single instance in which God took anything from Job. This is an important point in changing our overall viewpoint, our perspective of the book of Job. Let's look a little deeper.

Many have read **Job 1:21** and simply assumed Job knew exactly what he was talking about. If you listen to Christian radio you know that there have even been many songs written concerning this particular portion of scripture. Nevertheless, we need to go outside of the book of Job in order to build a proper foundation toward a correct understanding of this oldest book recorded in scripture.

"All scripture is given by inspiration of God, and is profitable for doctrine, for reproof, for correction, for instruction in righteousness:" 2 **Timothy 3:16**

In *2* **Timothy 3:16** we see why the book of Job appears in the Bible: for understanding (instruction). A proper understanding of Job will allow us to see many things in a different light. One of the most important areas comes in dealing with difficult times in our life or the life of another.

We have many advantages over Job and all of the other people who lived prior to the New Covenant, which we now live under, not the least of which is our salvation. Job was *not* born again! This may come as a tremendous surprise to many, but Job did not have a savior as you and I do in this New Covenant day and age.

Job also had absolutely no revelation of the Devil. If you search the entire book of Job, you will not find a single instance where Job, his first wife nor any of his friends ever mentioned Satan. That is due to the fact that they had no clue of such a being. That also meant that they did not have authority over Satan as you and I do today (**Luke 9:1**).

Job was very much aware of God but as far as he knew, God was the only power in existence. He had no reason to believe in any other Being that could have been the root cause of his problems. If he had known of Satan, he may have said, "the Lord gives and Satan takes away". Job was truly at a disadvantage when compared to the New Covenant believer (you and I) of today.

Upon further research we will see that Satan was mentioned a total of 18 times in the Old Testament portion of the Bible. Fourteen of those instances can be found in the book of Job, none of which come from Job, neither his wife nor any of his friends, as mentioned earlier. However, Satan is mentioned 35 times in the New Testament, and referred to by many of its different writers.

There are other areas where you will find Satan referred to as the Devil as well as other terms. For the sake of the topic of this book, we will not go into the other areas and names by which Satan is referenced in the Bible.

Another key point is that Satan is only mentioned in the book of Job between chapters one and two but not in any other place throughout its 42 chapters. Had Job or any of the others known of Satan they could have mentioned him as the true culprit behind Job's struggles.

As we look back at **Job 1:21** we can now draw the proper conclusion. It is true that Job made the statement, *"the Lord gave and the Lord has taken away"*. However, upon further inspection we see that it was not God but rather Satan who actually took from Job. You may now say, "I see that it was Satan who took from Job but God is the one who allowed him to do it".

There are several different perspectives of this viewpoint. The most popular is the belief that God is the one who allowed Satan to attack and steal from Job. There is also a belief that Job was a fearful man and his fear opened the door to the attacks from Satan. We will investigate what allowed Satan to do what he did in chapter three.

Chapter 3

Dissecting the Book of Job

I do not plan to dissect the book of Job verse by verse. We would end up with a book containing as many pages as the Bible itself or more! However, I am going to hit on some key verses that will help shed some light on this fascinating book.

Job chapter 1:1-7

"There was a man in the land of Uz, whose name was Job; and that man was perfect and upright, and one that feared God, and eschewed evil. 2 And there were born unto him seven sons and three daughters. 3 His substance also was seven thousand sheep, and three thousand camels, and five hundred yoke of oxen, and five hundred she asses, and a very great household; so that this man was the greatest of all the men of the east. 4 And his sons went and feasted in their houses, every

one his day; and sent and called for their three sisters to eat and to drink with them. 5 And it was so, when the days of their feasting were gone about, that Job sent and sanctified them, and rose up early in the morning, and offered burnt offerings according to the number of them all: for Job said, It may be that my sons have sinned, and cursed God in their hearts. Thus did Job continually. 6 Now there was a day when the sons of God came to present themselves before the LORD, and Satan came also among them. 7 And the LORD said unto Satan, Whence comest thou? Then Satan answered the LORD, and said, From going to and fro in the Earth, and from walking up and down in it."

This is where most people start to get into the wrong mindset concerning Job and the events surrounding his life as we see it in the Bible. In the verses leading up to verse 8, we are offered some insight into Jobs life: who he was, where he was from, and how he was viewed. As we read on, we learn about his family and possessions. If we back up to verse 4, we will see a key factor concerning Job. This key factor has to do with his sons and daughters and the way they conducted themselves.

Verse 4 reveals that Job was a man of fear. His regular habit was to make burnt offerings on their (his children's) behalf, He did so on a regular basis which is an indicator of his fear on their behalf. Many believers will jump to chapter 3 to say that Job's fear is what opened the door to Satan:

"For the thing which I greatly feared is come upon me, and that which I was afraid of is come unto me." Job 3:25

In our day and age, we live under the New Covenant: a time in which fear will most certainly open the door to Satan. Nevertheless, as we will soon see, it did not matter what Job did. Satan had an open door, under the Old Covenant, PERIOD*!*

As we continue to read toward verse 8, we see that Satan had entered into the Lord's presence upon which God asked him: *"why are you here?"* **Job 1:7**. Satan answered the Lord by saying that he had been roaming about in the Earth. The easiest way to interpret Satan's answer is to conclude that he was scheming and or planning. What was he planning? He was planning an attack on Job's life. Now we reach verse 8:

"And the LORD said unto Satan, Hast thou considered my servant Job, that there is none like him in the Earth, a perfect and an upright man, one that feareth God, and escheweth evil?"

If we read verse 8 purely on a surface level it appears that God is setting up a battle in which Job is the pawn. However, this is not the case. When God said, *"have you considered my servant Job?"*, He was most certainly not looking for information from Satan. He was doing what many parents do when they know that their kids have been sneaking cookies out of the cookie jar without first asking permission.

The most accurate translation of the Old Testament portion of the Bible is found in its original language, which is the Hebrew language. When we read **Job 1:8** as it is written in the Hebrew translation, it puts a completely new spin on the book of Job. The Hebrew translation of **Job 1:8** reads as follows: "*Why* *have you set your heart upon my servant, Job?"* <u>WHAT A CONTRAST</u>! Now we can continue to research the book of Job from a completely different frame of mind concerning all that we are about to see: A new perspective*!*

If a parent knows that his child has been sneaking cookies out of the cookie jar without permission they may ask a question like, "have you considered taking a cookie out of the cookie jar?" In this instance, the parent is not really seeking an answer because they already know the answer. They are merely letting the child know that they are on to them! You may call it "shock value" as a look of shock will come across the child's face while he or she thinks, "How did they know I have been sneaking cookies?" God was using the same tactic to let Satan know that He was fully aware of what was taking place. God was using "shock value" in this situation.

"Then Satan answered the LORD, and said, Doth Job fear God for nought? 10 Hast not thou made an hedge about him, and about his house, and about all that he hath on every side? thou hast blessed the work of his hands,

and his substance is increased in the land. 11 But put forth thine hand now, and touch all that he hath, and he will curse thee to thy face. 12 And the LORD said unto Satan, Behold, all that he hath is in thy power; only upon himself put not forth thine hand. So Satan went forth from the presence of the LORD."

In verses 9 through 11 Satan is trying to manipulate God. He was trying his best to have God do what he himself wanted to do. However, since God was already aware of Satan's plan He simply stated a fact in verse 12: *"And the LORD said unto Satan, Behold, all that he hath is in thy power"*. God was not giving Satan "control" over Job and his life. *Satan already had control over those things!* This may cause some confusion so let's step back and see how and why Satan had control over Job's life and possessions.

In order to gain an understanding of how Satan managed to gain control, over not only Job but also the entire Earth, we need to look to the book of Genesis. When God created man, He did not intend to run man's life for him. In our day and age, modern thought would call this being "sovereign". Instead, God *gave control* of the Earth to man in Genesis chapter 1:26.

"And God said, Let us make man in our image, after our likeness: and let them have dominion over the fish of the sea, and over the fowl of the air, and over the cattle, and over all the Earth, and over every creeping thing that creepeth upon the Earth."

The word **dominion** is defined as, *the power or right of governing and controlling.* Needless to say, God gave man control over the Earth.

In essence, man was free to do as he wished. However, as we all know, God instructed Adam to *not* eat of "the tree of the knowledge of good and evil". We also know in retrospect, things did not turn out according to the way God instructed Adam and Eve. I don't have time to go into great detail concerning this topic. The reason I bring this information to your attention is so that we can see *how* and *why* Satan already had control over the Earth during Job's time.

When Eve took that bite out of the fruit and then shared it with Adam, the two of them had yielded their God given power over to Satan. This is when he took control over the Earth, *not* because God gave it to him, but because Man had yielded his God given power to the devil.

This is where the belief that Satan has to go to God to get permission for anything he does, most likely originated. In all reality, Satan already had control over the Earth and could have attacked Job, his life, and his possessions without "asking God for permission". Satan was convinced that he could attack Job and in turn get him, (Job) to turn from God and "*curse thee to thy face*". However, Satan was literally too dumb to realize that God was way ahead of him concerning the matter. God knew Job would never turn from Him but He also knew that Satan could attack him regardless because the New Covenant had not yet been made with man. Jesus had not yet come to the Earth to start the work of defeating Satan and giving all authority back to mankind. Satan was still in control*!*

From here, the events of Job's struggles began to unfold.

Chapter 4

One Man's Unenviable Story

We live in a world where envy tends to be a major issue. People envy everything from their neighbor's, car, home, job, and even their spouse. Obviously envy is not a good thing as seen in the Bible (**Acts 17:5, Romans 1:29**). However, there will never be a person who envies Job when it came to his difficulties.

We see the account of Job's unenviable troubles begin with **Job 1:13 – 22**.

It goes without saying that Job had just experienced the worst day of his life*!* After all, Job was a wealthy and successful man. As we see in our modern day, success and wealth do not come without hard work and perseverance. No doubt, Job had put a lot of time and effort into what he built and accumulated, but this would all pale in comparison to the tragedies he had just witnessed.

We have already discovered the lack of truth in Job's statement from **Job 1:21** *"the LORD* *gave, and the LORD hath taken away"*. Nevertheless, let's take a closer look at the next verse, **1:22**. What does this verse mean when it says, *"Job sinned not, nor charged God foolishly"?*

According to *Strong's Concordance* (***Hebrew 5414***) the word, "charged" means: *to add, apply, appoint, ascribe, assign.* In other words, Job was *not* putting the blame on God and assigning blame to God for what had just taken place*!* However, this is *not* how the majority of New Testament believers apply what they read in this verse of Job.

Instead, many will utter phrases such as: *"We don't know why God allowed this to happen"* or *"God is in control, everything happens for a reason"*. While Job did not have the same knowledge as you and I have today, he did not directly point his finger at God and blame Him for the horrible events that had taken place in his life.

One interesting side note: have you ever noticed that many people seldom say, "God is in control" or "Everything happens for a reason" unless something bad has taken place*?* Think about it. It's true*!* The large majority of people will seldom bring God into the picture unless something unpleasant has taken place. There may be some exceptions to this rule but they are far and few between. Nevertheless, many Christians still point to the book of Job when bad things take place.

As we move into chapter 2 we see a repeating pattern of events take place beginning with verses one through three

Obviously, I don't need to take the time and re-explain what **Job 2:3** means, as it is identical to **Job 1:8**. However, it is extremely important that we pay attention to the many variations of translation when reading the Bible. While I tend to stick to the King James more so than any other version of the Bible, there are always issues with "mans" interpretations. In addition, other translations often leave much to be desired. I am not against any version of the Bible but I do feel that some translations lead to more confusion than they do to clear answers.

This is evidenced by the way **Job 1:8** and **Job 2:3** read in the King James as opposed to what we see in the Hebrew translation of these same verses. I do believe that the Bible is so simple that we need the help of others to misunderstand it, and there are also some translations of God's Word that seem to create misunderstandings. I also believe that there is a degree of study required to begin to gain some proper understanding. Don't get me wrong. I'm not saying that we can figure it all out. However, we *can* learn more and more as we take advantage of simple, yet important tools such as a concordance and a dictionary.

A dictionary may sound like an odd tool to use for studying the Word of God but it is important for us to understand the meaning of the words we use and read today. We do this, so as not to misuse them and thereby misinterpret what Job, as well as the other books of the Bible are trying to communicate. For example, one of the most misused words in the church today is the word, *sovereign*. The New International Version (NIV) of the Bible has popularized this word, since 1973. The dictionary definition is very different when compared to the modern church's definition.

In **Job 2:4-6**, once again we see the same scenario as we did in chapter 1. Satan had come to God to do his best to tempt God to do what he (Satan) himself wanted to do. Let's face it; Satan was not too happy with God for obvious reasons and not very bright. Satan was dumb enough to think he could over power God.

Now, he has made an equally dumb choice when he tried to tempt God to cause destruction in Job's life; **"But put forth thine hand now, and touch his bone and his flesh, and he will curse thee to thy face" (2:5**). This will *not* be the last time Satan tries to "tempt" God*!*

Once again, God stated the obvious, as we discovered in chapter 1, by telling Satan, "*Job's life is already under your control*".

As we move on to verses seven through nine we see more problems coming Job's way. This time Satan smote Job's body with boils. After this takes place, we see something that sadly, resembles modern day Christianity: someone believes that God is responsible for the bad things that take place in the lives of people.

Job 2:9, *"Then said his wife unto him, Dost thou still retain thine integrity? curse God, and die."*

Job's wife was blaming God for what happened. This is exactly what most of us have done at some point or another. We have a bad experience that may be contrary to something we have been praying for, or an unexpected bad experience may take place. This is when the distorted "Sovereignty of God" doctrine tends to rear its ugly head.

While Job's wife may have wanted him to pin his problems on God, Job himself refused to do so! *Job 2:10, " But he said unto her, Thou speakest as one of the foolish women speaketh. What? shall we receive good at the hand of God, and shall we not receive evil? In all this did not Job sin with his lips."*

Most of us have faced what we considered to be dire circumstances, and no doubt they were (are). However, I'm quite sure they would not hold a candle to Job's experiences, yet many still try to lay the responsibility on God when bad things happen. I can remember times when I was younger when I would have a contrary experience to what I wanted and would say "If God had wanted to stop this or that from happening He could have"! Of course, I know now that I was completely wrong!

The Bible tells us that it is our decisions and the way we think that determines how our life will go (**see Proverbs 19:3, Proverbs 23:7**).

Chapter 5

Good Friends or a Bad Influence?
———— W ————

As is the case with most successful and wealthy people, Job had "friends". However, his friends were not exactly the type of people I would want coming to my aid during any sort of crisis. We pick up their introduction in *Job 2:11-13*.

Can you imagine trying to comfort a person who has had the experiences of Job? Most of us would fall apart like a Ford Model A, trying to race on a set of railroad tracks.

We have already looked at the fact that Job did not curse God nor charge Him with his experiences. Nevertheless, that does not mean that Job didn't get angry with God. It's possible for us to be angry with someone but not charge him or her with what has taken place in a given situation. We will begin to see some interesting patterns emerge as we move into chapter 3 of Job. Some of what we are about to discuss reminds me a lot of the reactions of many modern-day Christian.

One thing I used to struggle with was being a chronic complainer. I would complain about pretty much anything and everything. The thing I failed to realize for many years was the fact that my complaints never brought about any positive change. Job's own words in **Job 3:20-26** provide a great example.

There are many views of the book of Job and why he dealt with such dire circumstances. One of the more common views as to why Satan was able to do what he did to Job is that Job's fear opened the door.

I must admit that I once had this very view myself. However, over the years as I have studied the book of Job, I have come to realize that fear was not the *main* issue. I do believe that Job's fear didn't help the situation by any means. However, it was not the sole cause as to what allowed Satan to cause such destruction in his life.

The common view concerning Job's fear comes primarily from two verses: **Job 1:5** and **3:26**.

Fear is much like the scent of a bleeding animal to a predator. It attracts from miles*!*

Job's fear, no doubt got the attention of Satan but it was what Job had that made Satan decide to target him in the first place.

You see, Satan was not pleased with God since He had given him the left foot of fellowship right out of Heaven. In return, Satan wanted to get back at God in some way, shape or form. He was attempting to do so with Job. As we have already seen, Satan tried to manipulate God into doing to Job what he himself wanted to do. Satan knew if he could make God "*touch all that Job had*", he could sit back and poke fun at God for causing destruction to one of His own children who had ultimately done nothing wrong. However, God was very much aware of what was taking place and would not fall for such trickery. We should learn from this and not fall into similar traps. Remember, Satan only has one weapon and one weapon only: deceit!

Deceit comes in many forms and from many venues. One of the most common venues of deceit in our lives can come from misinformed friends, as was the case with Job.

In Job chapter 4, we see the first of several accounts in which Job's friends spoke their mind. As we have already read in the preceding verse, Job's friends were **Eliphaz, Bildad, and Zophar.** *Eliphaz* was obviously the leader. We see him speak up in four separate chapters in the book of Job, (chapters 4 & 5, 15, and 22).

One of the worst misconceptions made by Christians is to take anything that is written in scripture and build doctrine out of it. We have already looked at the fact that all scripture is to be used for the purpose of "learning". In many cases, we can learn what not to do!

The reason I bring this up is due to what we will see later in Job 42, where God rebukes Eliphaz and his two friends. God deals directly with Eliphaz and tells him, *"You have not spoken of me what is true"*. Some of what Eliphaz and his friends said held water but the *majority* of their claims line up with modern day religion, *not* with the truth of God's Word. Therefore, we need to be cautious in how we apply what we read in their accounts. We will talk a lot more about what happened in Job 42 and why it took place at the end of this book.

As we have seen, Job and his friends sat without speaking a word for a solid week to one another, but Job's anger sparked a change in the atmosphere. While his friends did no wrong in coming against Job's anger, they were completely wrong to claim that it was God who was to blame for what was taking place in Job's life. This information can be found in **Job 4:1-6**.

Eliphaz was laying a foundation for what he was about to say in the next few verses, and these verses remind me of what is common in many of our modern-day churches. Any time there is some sort of bad situation that arises, it seems many people are ready and quick to blame God!

In **Job 4:7-11**, Eliphaz was proclaiming that Job had experienced the judgment of God. This is also common in the modern day church but there is one *major* difference. For those of us who hear similar "explanations", we also hear these folks quoting Old Testament scriptures from a time in which God's judgment <u>was</u> being poured out upon mankind. Keep in mind, those who lived in Job's day did not have a Bible to read. We are far ahead of them yet they pointed the finger at God in the same manner as many still do in our day and age, under the New Covenant.

I believe the answer for this false blame game, is simple. **John 10:10** tells us, "the *thief comes only to steal and kill and destroy*". The thief referred to in **John 10:10** is none other than the Devil himself. Satan was obviously alive and well during the days of Job and his friends, and his intentions were no different than they are today. He wanted to disgrace God*!*

I know many of us may not like what I am about to say but it is necessary. We have all had experiences in which we were "used of God" in a given situation. In the same way that we can be used of God and not even know it, we can also be used of the Devil and not know it. It all depends on what we are opening ourselves up to. We are not going to go into detail as to how this works because if we did, I would end up writing two books instead of one.

The reason I bring this point up, is that Eliphaz was being used of the Devil to point the finger at God as the one who was to blame for what Job had experienced.

The next few verses in Job 4 will reveal some insight into Eliphaz and his way of thinking. Remember, just because it appears in scripture does not mean we need to apply it personally in our day-to-day lives as if what is said is set in stone as being from and of God.

Job 4:12, "Now a thing was secretly brought to me, and mine ear received a little thereof."

Here Eliphaz was attempting to strengthen his argument concerning what he had just said to Job. This falls right in line with what takes place among many Christians in our day and age. A Christian who has a distorted view of God will go to great lengths to strengthen their point. Some will even go to the point of yelling and screaming at the top of their lungs. If you want to know who has a distorted view of God, simply tell any group of "Christians" that God is _not_ angry. Whoever "gets angry" has just revealed their perception of God.

As for Eliphaz, he began to speak of a vision he had *which he believed* was from God. The vision was more than likely something that had come to him in previous days or even a period beyond just a few days.

When we look into other areas of Old Testament scripture, we see that others needed someone to interpret their dreams for them. I believe this is an important point; it is likely that Eliphaz was speaking based on his own interpretation of his vision. This vision obviously *not* from God simply because of the fact that it condemned Job. This may be a revelation for some of you; not all visions are from God!

Something we seem to forget and or not recognize is that God is not the only spirit vying for our attention. Many people will speak out in the name of God and claim they have a word directly from Him. The problem is that these supposed "words from the Lord" might not line up with scripture.

Galatians 1:8-9, "Let God's curse fall on anyone, including us or even an angel from heaven, who preaches a different kind of Good News than the one we preached to you. 9 I say again what we have said before: If anyone preaches any other Good News than the one you welcomed, let that person be cursed." (NLV)

We need to make sure that what is said to be of God truly lines up with the Bible. There is no substitute, period! Many in the modern day church have strayed away from using the Bible as a standard of weights and measures to make sure what they believe is of God, is truly from God and not a lie from the Devil. Sadly, many

Christians do not want to slow down long enough to research the Bible and make sure what they heard or saw in a vision or any other method of delivery is something that can be accurately backed up within scripture.

This reminds me of a time when I was speaking to a local pastor in my city. I knew this man and I had heard of his desire to see miracles taking place within his church. I was really excited to hear this because there are many pastors out there who do not believe in miracles today.

One day I was out walking and saw him at the end of his driveway. I stopped by and began to talk to him concerning this matter of seeing miracles. In our conversation, I mentioned that we needed to learn to look at healing the same way as we view salvation. When I said this, I meant that we needed to view healing as a completed work just as we view salvation. When we lead a person in the prayer of salvation, for example, we do not believe that God *can* save them but we believe it is already a completed work of the cross, which was fulfilled by Christ. It's a done deal*!* According to scripture, healing is the same*!* **1 Peter 2:24** tells us that we are already healed by the stripes of Jesus. In Colossians, Paul tells us to walk by faith in all areas just as we did when we received Christ.

Colossians 2:6, "As ye have therefore received Christ Jesus the Lord, so walk ye in him."

When we became born again, we did not base that experience on one of our five senses. We became born again by grace, through faith. We are to continue to walk in Christ the same way we became born again. Salvation, "sozo" includes forgiveness of our sin, yet also provides for our finances, healing, deliverance, relationships, and any other area we may have a need.

After I had made the statement to this pastor that we needed to look at healing the same way as we looked at salvation, he proceeded to tell me that it is not *always* "God's will" to heal. In turn, I asked him on what scripture he based his beliefs concerning healing. He didn't quote a single scripture but rather told me that he had prayed with a large number of people and not all of them had been healed. He was basing his beliefs on something other than scripture. In fact, in so many words, he told me that he based his belief of healing on his experiences and *not* the Bible.

On the other hand, if he had taken any of the experiences he had when he prayed for others and filtered them through the Word of God, his beliefs probably would have been different. He could have seen scriptures such as **Isaiah 53:5**, **Acts 10:38**, and **1 Peter 2:24** that speak of God's will for healing, from a different vantage point. We are not going to take the time to discuss this topic in depth in this book, but I encourage you to look these scriptures up on your own. The reason I bring this point up is due to Eliphaz' strong desire to filter his view of his vision through his own beliefs. He never sought any other counsel that we know of, nor did he ask God what the dream meant. I know this is not clearly stated in scripture, but when we research the rest of the book of Job, we will see that his interpretation of the vision does not line up with God's true nature.

Job 4:13, "In thoughts from the visions of the night, when deep sleep falleth on men," . . .

A vision of the night is no different from a dream. Dreams are often referred to as visions in other areas of scripture.

The "fear" caused by the dream is a great indicator that it was *not* from or of God. This dream was so frightening that it made Eliphaz' hair stand on end! (*Job 4:14-18*)

This is similar to what the narrator of the book of Job cited as being Job's fault in **Job 32:2**. Therefore, we can draw the conclusion that there was a small amount of truth to what Eliphaz was saying. However, the mistake Eliphaz made was to claim that Job's troubles were due to God's judgment. Does that sound familiar? Even under the New Covenant, many people will proclaim God's judgment over a person or event, even a nation when bad things happen.

One great point made by Eliphaz was in verse 18. He was saying that angels are absolutely nothing when compared to the Lord. Thus Eliphaz questions, who was Job to think that he could reprove God?

When all is said and done, I could write an entire book about Eliphaz. He is somebody we can learn from but we don't want to follow in his footsteps. In fact, he is a great example to learn from so that we don't make the same mistakes as he did. The Bible is very clear about learning by example as opposed to experience.

I am sure we can all remember a time when we have heard our parents say, "I just don't want you to learn the hard way". Believe it or not, that is a God-like trait.

1 Corinthians 10:6 & 11, "Now these things were our examples, to the intent we should not lust after evil things, as they also lusted."

" Now all these things happened unto them for examples: and they are written for our admonition, upon whom the ends of the world are come."

While Paul was using the Israelites as an example for the Corinthians, the same thing applies to us as well. We are to learn by example and not by experience alone, in many areas of life. While we need to learn to drive a car by hands on experience, we can learn by example of what not to do such as running a red light. If we see a person run a red light and have an accident, we can say, "I don't want to do that". In such a case, we have learned by example. Another good way to put this is to say we don't want to spend any more time in the "school of hard knocks" than we absolutely have to.

When we look at Eliphaz, we are looking at someone from whom we can learn. Let's just learn to do the opposite!

Chapter 6

Let God be True and Every Man a Liar

Romans 3:4 says, *"Let God be true and every man a liar."*

When we step back and allow God to show the difference between truth and tradition we are bound to see things as they really are. Man's view of the book of Job has been based on what is seen on the surface. As we have already pointed out, what goes on below the surface will tell the truth of a situation as opposed to what we are seeing on top of the surface. Many of the verses in the book of Job have not only been used to point the finger at God as the reason why bad things happen, but also to back up other wrong beliefs.

Job 5:1, "Call now, if there be any that will answer thee; and to which of the saints wilt thou turn?"

Many have used what Eliphaz said in **Job 5:1** to justify *"calling on saints"* as is a common practice in the Catholic Church.

The reason I bring this particular verse out is to prove a point. That point is to take God's Word over any man's word. That includes my word! You may not agree with what I am saying in this book. If that is the case, you need to go directly to God and ask Him to show you the truth. That doesn't mean you should go about discovering the difference between right and wrong by using the same scripture verses you have in the past. Trusting in God will lead us to new eye-opening revelations. We don't need to hear only what man has to say but we need to go to the Word of God for confirmation.

Most people will understand and agree with the point I have made concerning the fact that it was Satan who took from Job, not God. However, they also utter a common statement: **"Satan may have been the one who took from Job, but God allowed it"**. This is particularly what I want to deal with in the remainder of this book.

I once had a person who commented on a video in which I mentioned the fact that God does not do bad things to us. He came against the fact that I said God is not doing bad things to any of His children in our day and age: the New Covenant. He cited the book of Job as a way to proclaim that God will take things from us as retribution due to sin in our lives. This of course goes completely against what Jesus came to accomplish. You see, Jesus stood in the gap for us, **(1 John 2:2)** and became a sacrifice in our place. Obviously, Jesus had not yet come on the scene during Job's lifetime. However, that does not mean that the reason for Job's troubles had anything to do with judgment.

Please allow me to take a short but necessary rabbit trail with this line of thinking.

Under the Old Covenant, God was dealing with man based on what man deserved. In other words, God was imputing (charging) man's sins directly to man. However, we do not live under the Old Covenant in any way, shape, or form.

2 Corinthians 5:19, "To wit, that God was in Christ, reconciling the world unto himself, not imputing their trespasses unto them; and hath committed unto us the word of reconciliation."

The word, reconciliation, means to "become friendly with" or "to make right". The word, impute, is an accounting term, which means, "to charge to".

It is safe to say that God, through Jesus' sacrifice on the cross in our place, has become friendly with us and is not charging our sins to our accounts.

Obviously, there had not been a sacrifice for Job to call upon, as we have in the form of

51

Jesus; even the Old Covenant had not yet been established. Nevertheless, that does not mean that any of Job's problems have a single thing to do with God's judgment upon his life. In **Job 1:8** God said, *"that there is none like him in the Earth, a perfect and an upright man, one that feareth God, and escheweth evil?"* God looked at Job as being a good man, not a terrible person worthy of judgment. It is very important that we realize that Job's problems had nothing to do with any part of God's plan for his life. Any problems we deal with concerning Satan in our own lives are also not a part of God's plan for us.

As we move forward into Job chapter 5, we will see that Job's children had been destroyed in one quick moment. Therefore, Eliphaz was comparing Job to a foolish man of sin, whose children had been destroyed as payment for his sins (**Job 5:2-5**). We have already established the fact that this was simply not the case.

Eliphaz actually made an accurate statement in **Job 5:6** when he said that Job's problems were not just natural. Job's problems were no doubt created by the Devil with the intention to cause him to turn from God. This is something that the Devil tries with us as well. However, Eliphaz was not making this point for any other reason than to attempt to strengthen his earlier statements.

Job 5:7, " Yet man is born unto trouble, as the sparks fly upward."

There is no doubt that we are born into a fallen world. We can become born again, make all of the right choices in each situation we may face yet, still have problems. As long as we are living in this fallen world we will never live a problem-free life, but that does not mean our problems have a single thing to do with God's plan for us.

There is nothing wrong with understanding the fact that we will have problems, but to say that they are part of God's plan for our lives is complete foolishness. The Lord created us to live in paradise and if it had not been for sin entering into the world, via man's willingness to go against God's Word, that would still be the case. It is Satan who is the one who has come to steal, kill, and destroy **(John 10:10)**. All he needs is an open door from which he can enter into our lives and cause destruction, but *it is up to us* to open that door. God is *not* the one who chooses what Satan can or cannot do.

While Job did not have revelation of, or authority over the Devil, it was still man who opened the door for Satan to come and cause destruction in Job's life, as we point out in chapter 1 of Genesis.

God's original plan was for man to have full control over the Earth.

Genesis 1:26, " God said, Let us make man in our image, after our likeness: and let them have dominion over the fish of the sea, and over the fowl of the air, and over the cattle, and over all the Earth, and over every creeping thing that creepeth upon the Earth."

Genesis 1:28, " And God blessed them, and God said unto them, Be fruitful, and multiply, and replenish the Earth, and subdue it: and have dominion over the fish of the sea, and over the fowl of the air, and over every living thing that moveth upon the Earth."

In these verses found in **Genesis 1:26** and **28** we see God giving man control over the Earth. The words, dominion and subdue, both mean "to take control of". God was telling man "<u>you</u> are in control of the Earth".

God never takes back His words nor makes any changes to what He has already put in place.

Psalm 89:34, " My covenant will I not break, nor alter the thing that is gone out of my lips."

God did not take back control of the Earth when man gave it away **(Genesis chapter 3)**. Instead, He sent Jesus to defeat the Devil and give authority over the Earth back to mankind.

Eliphaz may have given good advice in **Job 5:8** but it is always easy to do so when we are not the one who is going through the difficult time. In addition, Eliphaz did make a true statement concerning God in *Job 5:9* when he said, *" Which doeth great things and unsearchable; marvellous things without number."*

However, when we move forward to **Job 5:16** we will see an event that some of us have dealt with in the modern day church.

Job 5:16, "So the poor hath hope, and iniquity stoppeth her mouth."

Eliphaz had been trying to make a point to Job concerning the fact that God is a just God. Obviously he was correct to note that God's true nature involves being just. God defends those who are pure in heart and He destroys the wicked. This was a truthful line of thinking but for Eliphaz to condemn Job, as being wicked was completely out of line**, judgmental** and inaccurate.

Job 5:17, "Behold, happy is the man whom God correcteth: therefore despise not thou the chastening of the Almighty."

In **Job 5:17** Eliphaz was proclaiming that all of the tragedy in Job's life was a direct result of

God's correction. Again, does this sound familiar? This is a very common thought process acted upon in modern day Christianity in which the book of Job is used as the foundation. However, just as was the case with Eliphaz, this is a completely wrong conclusion. Our problems, no matter how big or small, do not have any sort of redemptive power. Sure, we may learn from our mistakes and wrong reactions to given situations, but that does not mean that this situation took place because God allowed or caused it to happen.

The events in Job's life did not occur to make him become more like God or to smooth out any rough edges. This was not correction from God. Just as is the case for us today, God corrects via His Word, according to **2 Timothy 3:16**. In our case, we have a Bible to read, but Job did not have that advantage. However, before we complete our study of the book of Job, we will see how God dealt with all of the wrong views and accusations aimed in His direction. One of the most important nuggets we can garner from **Job 5:17** is the fact that those who teach that all of our problems are God's correction, are simply wrong, just as Job's friends were wrong. Eliphaz then continued in **Job 5:18** with his rant proclaiming that all of Job's problems were for the purpose of a God given correction.

2 Timothy 3:16, "All scripture is given by inspiration of God, and is profitable for doctrine, for reproof, for correction, for instruction in righteousness."

Obviously, God wants us to learn by simply reading His Word, **1 Cor. 10:6** and **11**. All scripture is to be used for the purpose of correction and instruction (to learn from). The book of Job is one of the absolute best books in the Bible, from which to learn. Sadly, many have missed the whole point of the book of Job and have used it as a foundation to create wrong doctrine. **Job 5:19** is a great example of this.

"He shall deliver thee in six troubles: yea, in seven there shall no evil touch thee."

Here Eliphaz was attempting to convince Job to humble himself and admit he had done something wrong to bring all of these problems upon himself. The point was that Job needed to admit wrongdoing and then God would instantly deliver him from all of his problems. If Job had truly been under the judgment of God, this way of thinking would have benefited Job, but Job was not under God's judgment by any means. Remember, God saw Job as being a "perfect and upright" man **(Job 1:8)**.

Eliphaz went onto proclaim that Job would receive the blessings of God *if* he was worthy of them. This is not true! None of us, including Job, gets what we deserve. If Job had been experiencing punishment from God, his problems would have been much worse.

Job 5:22 also reminds me of modern viewpoints concerning God. Many believe that God blesses us and will be involved in our lives based upon our individual performance. Many still believe this today.

Again, Eliphaz was assuming that Job's problems were a direct result of poor performance in the sight of the Lord. We have already examined the fact that God did not view Job as being a wicked man. In turn, we can assume that Job's problems were not due to God's plan for his life by any means. This is why it is so important for us to change our viewpoint and make sure we are looking things over from multiple directions so as not to miss anything.

Eliphaz may have meant well by what he was saying to Job. However, good intentions of the heart do not make what we say automatically right. In order for Job to give in and admit that Eliphaz was right in what he was saying, Job would have needed to lie. He would have had to admit to committing sins, which he had not committed. However, Job knew better and refused to lie and give in just to satisfy his friends.

We can all learn from this particular instance. We have all faced different situations in which we just wanted to get people off our backs for one reason or another. In some cases, we have lied and acted as if what they were telling us was correct. While such an act may free us from having to deal with that person for the moment, it does not open the door to God in our lives.

Chapter 7

Job Responds

We have been looking at the comments made by Eliphaz toward Job. Obviously, Eliphaz meant well in all he was saying to Job but as I have already mentioned, good intentions do not always equal correct knowledge. As you will see, I am slowly building to a specific point in order to show that *God* was absolutely *not* the reason for Job's troubles. Job begins his response in *Job 6:1-4*.

Job will end up responding many times before the book of Job has reached its conclusion. I am not going to discuss each place where Job responds to what his friends have said to him. If you wish to research these areas on your own, you will find them in Job chapters 3, 6-7, 9-10, 12-14, 16-17, 19, 21, 23-24, and 26-31.

In this first instance, Job did not believe any of his friends could even begin to grasp what he was going through. Just as tends to be the case in many of our own life experiences, Job wanted to find a way to show his friends how bad things really were. It was his desire that they have a full understanding of his emotions and feelings. Job's grief was truly far greater than any words could possibly describe. If you have ever lost a loved one and had the experience of a well meaning but misinformed friend say, "I know how you feel", you can understand Job's plight. Sadly, Job shares the same opinion as Eliphaz in that he believes his troubles are due to the judgment of God. However, unlike Eliphaz, Job does not believe this supposed judgment is due to any great sin. This is the point where Job begins to defend himself and condemn God.

Job 6:5, "Doth the wild ass bray when he hath grass? or loweth the ox over his fodder?"

Job was saying that no noise is ever made without proper justification. In other words, Job is saying that he is justified to complain to God based upon his experiences. He believed that it was God who had caused the events he had experienced. Of course, this simply is not true but it is how Job saw things, his perspective from the front view of the car so-to-speak.

Many times, we will hear people defend themselves or others by saying, "that is just how I or they understand it to be". Our understanding may not be correct in many cases and we are never justified to respond in improper ways. Just because we have been taught that it is okay to steal a little money from petty cash does not make it okay to commit theft. Does that make sense? There are many other examples I could use but the bottom line is simple; our understanding of how and why things should be done a certain way does not justify us continuing with wrong behavior patterns. Job had absolutely no justification to condemn God but in his own mind, it was perfectly okay to do so, and as we have just pointed out, that does not make it okay by any means.

In **Job 6:8**, Job says that he wishes to simply die and be finished with his difficult circumstances. In essence, Job was looking for the easiest way out. If any of us ever long for death, we are surely taking the wrong path. This is not a Godly desire to say the least and we would be way off course if we reached such a place. The right thing to do in such a situation is to backtrack and figure out where and why, or *if* we missed the mark. This is not about condemnation but about figuring out how to properly renew our mind and get back on track with God, or to stay the course and not allow these circumstances to derail our journey with Father. The problem is never on God's end, it is always on our end, or simply a ploy of our enemy, as in Job's case*!*

Job was not the type to attempt suicide. Instead, he was simply asking God to do the job for him. Obviously, most of us will never face anything even close to what Job went through. Our life situations are far different in many ways than they were during Job's lifetime.

At this point it is obvious that all of Job's strength and will to live are gone **(Job 6:11)**. From his point of view, he has no good reason to continue with the remainder of his life. This is much like what we experience when we are focused on ourselves and allow our natural circumstances to rule our emotions. This is very dangerous ground on which to stand. When we allow selfishness to birth thoughts of not wanting to continue in life, we are opening a wide open door to the Devil.

If we are willing to be honest, this is the time when things worsen for us. I know this well as I have been down this particular road in the past and it is not a pleasant place to spend any amount of time.

There were many times in years past when I behaved as a very selfish person. When things went south, I would tend to want my own life to end. In reality, I was completely focused on myself and not anyone else. It is amazing how things can change for us when we focus outwardly, rather than inward, but this is not what Job was doing in chapter 6.

There is no doubt that we are the ones who choose how we react to given situations we may face. Obviously, the more difficult things we experience the more of a challenge a right reaction can be. One of the best things that can happen to us when dealing with difficult circumstances is to be blessed with the company of good, Godly friends. They can help build us back up with encouragement and reminders of what we truly know about the faithfulness and goodness of God. However, in Job's situation, he found very little comfort from these three friends. The events I am speaking of continue in **Job 6:14-17**.

Job was not pleased with his friends and what he viewed as their lack of pity towards him. Let's face it, if we were in the middle of difficult times and our friends came along and began accusing us of forsaking God, we would not be very pleased with them ourselves. At least Job did recognize the error of his three friends' judgment.

In *Job 6:15*, Job is accusing his friends of being crooked. He realizes that his friends have been deceitful. This is something that we ourselves need to be aware of as well. The potential exists in the modern day church for our own friends to come to us in difficult times with information in err just as Job dealt with.

If God is really the reason why we go through difficult times, why should our friends ever come to comfort us? In doing so, they may negate God's plan for our lives by making us feel better. I know this may sound outrageous but if God is the reason why bad things happen to us, it must be his will for those things to take place. We would be better off to simply lie down and let our struggles have their full and intended effect in our lives. Of course, this is not true but I will deal with this particular area in a later chapter.

In **Job 6:17** we see the truth of what wrong knowledge, concerning why we deal with difficult times, will do to make us even more unhappy then we may be already. Job was comparing his friends to water, in that while it may be able to satisfy for a time, the satisfaction it gives is only temporary. This is why it is so important that we understand that God is never the reason for the struggles we may deal with in our lives no matter how big or small they may be.

Job never asked his friends to come and be part of his time of mourning **(Job 6:22-23)**. Eliphaz had condemned Job by proclaiming that God's judgment was upon him in the form of the events he had recently experienced. Job knew that words carried power but he was wise enough to reject the words spoken from Eliphaz.

The situation that Job dealt with really does take place today. Well meaning friends come to our aid, with the misunderstanding that God is the reason for our struggles. We may be in the midst of our pain and be weak when they make this approach. We may know in our heart that we haven't sinned against God but it is very easy to fall into the trap of the flesh and begin to question God. Job was wise enough not to do so. Job challenged the words of his friends, as he was very much aware that he hadn't done anything wrong.

Job even began to ask his friends to drop their process of wrong thinking in **6:28**. He wants them to understand that he is not the type of person who would lie to them. While we do not have a time frame as to the length of the friendship between the four men, they obviously had some sort of history together. Otherwise, the three friends would have not come to Job's aid. I believe Job was simply trying to remind them of the fact that he had never lied to them before so why would he begin doing so now? This is seen in **Job 6:28-30**.

Job had been longing for death. He even took the same road some of us have taken whether it be in secret or in a setting in which we are talking to others. He was trying to justify his desire for death in **Job 7:2**. He used the fact that everyone has to die at some point in time. Job had even begun to believe that his friends might be correct; maybe his problems were due to sin.

"As a servant earnestly desireth the shadow, and as an hireling looketh for the reward of his work."

We know that the wages of sin is death **(Romans 6:23)**. Job simply wanted to collect what was coming to him. However, let's not forget, Job's problems were not due to his own sin. In fact, we can go back to our earlier review of the events that took place in Genesis chapter 3 in which man had sinned and given Satan control over the Earth. On one hand, we can say that Job's problems were indeed due to sin. On the other hand, we must realize that the sin was not his own but rather that of Adam and Eve.

This brings up a very important point for us to focus on. We live in a fallen world and inevitably, we are going to experience difficult times. We can make the absolute best choices each day but we cannot escape what surrounds us. While we have many advantages that Job did not have, such as a revelation of the Devil and our authority over him, we still live in a fallen world. As a result, we are going to face situations that we more than likely would rather not. Does this mean everything we face happens because God wants it to? The answer is no, but as I have already mentioned, I will deal with this topic in detail in a later chapter. Let's use a simple-to-understand illustration to amplify what I am saying.

If we were to make a visit to a dairy farm, we would more than likely take a walk around in the pasture. On this A- typical pasture, we are sure to find an expected environment. Let's just say that this particular environment will cause us to face some challenges due to things that "have fallen" much like the challenges we face due to living in a fallen world. If we spend enough time in the pasture, we will eventually step in some cow "patties". While this experience is not one we would desire, it is bound to happen in such an environment. Does that mean we should go to the farmer who owns the farm and ask him why he allowed such a thing to happen to us? No way! It was not his fault nor did he cause or allow the event to take place. It simply happened because we were in an environment in which the chances of stepping in a cow patty greatly increased. Similar to the unwanted situations we find ourselves in because of the fallen world in which we live.

Job did not understand the fact that he lived in what had become a "fallen world". He had experienced great success and could not understand why he was dealing with such suffering. He didn't have the many aids by which to study as we do today. He didn't have a Bible to read nor did he have the Holy Spirit to draw upon for answers **(John 14:26)**. Job wasn't even born again! That statement may take some time to sink in, but let's not forget, there was no Savior in Job's day. Jesus had not yet come.

The point is that Job did not realize that his problems were due to the fact that he lived in a fallen world in which man had given Satan control.

In **Job 7:2**, Job was expressing his displeasure concerning the fact that he could not die on the spot. He didn't want to continue to live in his current state. Much as is the case with us when we feel this way (I know not everyone has felt this way but some of us have). Job could not see any point in living another moment in such a difficult state. I know I could tell you about some of the hardships I have faced and you could share yours with me as well. Yours may be far worse than anything I have ever faced but that does not mean we should seek death to get away from the pain. In essence, this thought process shows a complete lack of faith in God, and a complete lack of understanding concerning His true nature. When we wish to die to get away from our problems, it shows that we don't believe God can change things and restore our joy. In fact, the real issue is that we must renew our own mind before we will see positive change take place in our circumstances.

Job also experienced the same scenario that we have all faced at one time or another. We see this in 7:4, where Job cannot even gain any comfort when he tries to sleep. He instead spends his nights tossing and turning just as most of us have at one time or another.

I know many people who can lay their head down on their pillow and fall asleep within seconds. However, I am not able to do this myself except on rare occasions. The reason is that I tend to think a lot when I first go to bed. I normally am not thinking thoughts of worry but my thoughts keep me awake anyway. When I finally begin to slow down and relax, I stop thinking about whatever is occupying my thoughts and go to sleep much easier. Job was obviously so consumed with what he had experienced that he could not experience a peaceful night's rest. I am not saying that Job was completely in the wrong for doing so but I do believe he could have leaned on God and experienced relief from his pain in a much quicker manner than he experienced.

Job 7:7, "O remember that my life is wind: mine eye shall no more see good."

This is another verse that many of us can identify with. When we are in the midst of painful circumstances, it can seem as if the best days of our lives are behind us. I want to encourage you to never believe that lie! At times, it may seem as if we will never see the joys we once knew in life, but that is simply not true. Our best days can always be ahead.

God doesn't desire us to live in seasons of happiness for a period and then go through sadness for the remainder of our lives. However, if we allow ourselves to become self centered we most certainly could have this very experience. The choice is ours. We may have to fight and claw our way back to being happy again but it is not out of reach at any time unless we ourselves allow it to be. According to **Proverbs 23:7,** it is the way we think that determines how we act and react in all situations. This does not just apply in difficult times but in the best times of our lives as well. God has given us more power over our own lives than anything else.

In the next few verses of chapter 7, Job continues his rant concerning his desire to see his end come swiftly. When we reach a point such as this, it becomes extremely difficult to see any good within our field of vision. If we allow it to be so, the rest of our life can seem completely hopeless. Job was deep into such a mindset in chapter 7.

Job refers back to the dream shared by Eliphaz in **7:14-16**. He had come to a place where he would much rather die than live. He essentially tells his three friends to leave him alone so he can die and end his nightmarish experience.

In **7:17,** Job continues to speak of his justification in wanting to die. He describes man in the most sorrowful of terms in an effort to belittle his own life. In simplest terms, Job was trying to say that the loss of his own life would mean nothing. However, in verse **7:18** things begin to get really interesting as Job stops directing his complaints toward his friends and redirects them toward God **(Job 7:18-21)**.

Job simply wanted to know why God has never taken notice of him. He then asks the Lord to forsake him and let him strangle to death on his own spit! Job was angry with God! I can remember times gone by, when I had yet to gain an understanding of God's true nature and the fact that He is *never* the reason why bad things happened in my life. It was in those times that I would be angry with God as well. I would often utter phrases such as, "God, if you had wanted to keep this from happening you could have". Of course, I have grown up since then and know better. Job goes on to admit that he is a sinner. However, let's not forget what we studied earlier. Job knew that his troubles did not come upon him because of his own sin. However, Job did ask what his sins had done to God in the first place. This is much like what we deal with in our own lives.

When we are facing difficult circumstances, we may reach a point in which it seems like things are not getting better no matter what we do. We may begin to question God and wonder what we did to deserve such an experience.

73

When we finally calm down and are willing to approach our situation from a mature perspective, we can usually look back to a reaction of our own choosing that either flat out caused the situation we are facing or made it far more difficult.

Some people may feel as if I am saying that it is always our choices that determine what happens in our lives. Let's not forget the example of living in a fallen world. We live with, work with, and are around other people on a regular basis. That means that their choices can have an effect on our lives even when it is not our own choice for such things to happen. It is at these times when our decisions and reactions become so crucial. If another has wronged us, we are the one who chooses how we are going to react in the given situation. We will either open the door to faith in God or to the flesh, and we all know who is waiting for us behind the door of the flesh.

Chapter 7 ends with Job asking God why He didn't accept his sacrifices. As we saw in chapter 1 verse 4, Job often made sacrifice offerings on behalf of his children. Based on events that had taken place, Job felt as if God must not have accepted his sacrifice offerings. Essentially, Job felt that his performance should have been enough to keep his children from harm. Of course, we live under the New Covenant, a time in which only Jesus' performance determines how God sees us. We do not make sacrifice offerings as Job did or those who lived under the Old Covenant. On a side note, let's not forget that Job's life was not lived during the Old Covenant. He and others like Noah, etc. up until Abraham did not have the same sort of covenant with God as those who we read about in other areas of the Old and New Testament.

You may still be shocked at the statement I made in the last portion of chapter 6. I said that Job did *not* live under the Old Covenant. Many may say, "But the book of Job appears several books after the Old Covenant instructions were given to Moses. This is true to the extent of the order in which the books appear in our Bible. However, it is not true as to the times and dates each book was actually written.

Most scholars believe that the book of Job was written before the law was given to Moses due to the complete absence of any reference of The Law, throughout all 42 chapters of Job. There is also missing, any reference to any sort of covenant between God and man.

Additionally, the timing of the Book of Job can be researched through the name of the place where Job lived: the land of Uz. Noah's son, Shem, had a grandson whose name was Uz. The land of Uz could have been named after this person, which would suggest that Job's lifetime was after the flood that took place during Noah's lifetime. If this information is accurate then it means that the book of Job is one of the oldest books, if not the oldest book in the Bible, as most scholars believe.

Some scholars have also said that the book of Job was the first book of the Bible to be written. This could explain why we never hear any reference to the Old Covenant, or the Law. The simple fact that Job's friends viewed his problems as being related to his own sin, yet never mentioned the law, is proof enough of the information mentioned above.

Chapter 8

Bildad Speaks Up

We have already heard quite a bit from Job's friend, Eliphaz. Nevertheless, what did his other two friends have to say? In chapter 8, we are going to begin hearing from Bildad the Shuhite. Bildad spoke up in three separate chapters during the book of Job: chapters 8, 18 and 25. We can view his commentary toward Job, in much the same manner as Eliphaz, in that he shares some information that is correct. However, for the most part, his view of God is not pointed in the right direction.

While Bildad also realizes that Job is focused on himself and not on God, he also makes the incorrect assessment of proclaiming that God was the reason for Job's problems. We see a lot of information in which Job is told that God was the source of his problems. As we have already discussed and will continue to see, God was not the reason for Job's problems.

Bildad begins speaking in **Job 8:4-5,** although he was coming at the situation from a different viewpoint than Eliphaz. While Eliphaz believed that Job's problems came upon him due to God's judgment upon his own sins, Bildad pointed the finger at Job's children as being the cause for what had taken place. While this line of thinking is also untrue, Bildad went on to say that it didn't matter whether the events took place because of Job's sin or the sin of his children, all Job needed to do was repent and God would fix everything for him.

This is why so many believers in the church today believe that any problem we have is somehow tied to sin in our lives. However, they have not realized that Jesus came to take on all of God's anger and wrath against sin **(1 John 2:2)**. Our desires change as a direct result of the new birth. Continuing to live the way we did prior to our new birth, will only serve to make our lives miserable as we fling the door open to the Devil. He will be able to run into our lives and cause as much destruction as he wishes. While there truly is a tremendous advantage to working at not living in sin as much as we possibly can, that does not mean that God loves us more if we sin any less. *Nothing* with God is based upon our own performance by any means*!*

Romans 10:3, "For they being ignorant of God's righteousness, and going about to establish their own righteousness, have not submitted themselves unto the righteousness of God."

This verse makes it quite clear that we cannot do anything to establish our own righteousness. As I have already mentioned, many believe that any problems in our lives no matter how big or small they may be, are from God and intended to make us repent (turn around) from that sin. Many will cite the Old Testament law and then tie it into the book of Job, but there are several problems with that way of thinking. First, the Old Covenant Law was not yet established during Job's lifetime. Secondly, the law was never given to be used as a standard by which God judged mankind to determine if they were worthy or unworthy. In fact, the law was not given for God's purpose at all. It was given solely to show mankind that they could not live up to the impossible standard of the law. I am not going to go into detail of what those standards were but if you would like to research the law, you will find it written in detail throughout the books Exodus, Numbers and Deuteronomy, three of the first five books in the Bible.

It is very important that we understand why the law was given, so that we don't try to hang what happens in our lives on our performance as viewed by God. It may not always seem like God is blessing us. However, the Bible declares clearly that we have already been blessed with ALL spiritual blessings in Christ **(Ephesians 1:3)**. Some may argue this point and say, "that doesn't mean Earthly blessings". However, by **Ephesians 1:3** saying that we have been blessed with all "spiritual" blessings in Christ, it is simply representative of the fact that Jesus has made the way for us in all areas.

When we become born again, it is our spirit that is renewed. This verifies why we still tend to struggle so much in the fleshly areas of our lives. We are a three part being: spirit, soul, and body. One third of us changes when we become born again but that leaves two thirds flesh *that need to be renewed to this new way of living* to fight against the spiritual part of us which has been renewed. Remember our fight is NOT against flesh & blood. The Word of God instructs us, to believe what we read in scripture by *faith*, which means we may not be able to see instantly what the Bible says we have or can do, but we believe what it says, by *faith!* That is because these things are held in the spiritual realm until we, by *faith*, allow them to be released into the physical realm. Again, this is another topic for another book but it is a point we need to work on grasping in order to understand God's ways of dealing with us.

It is more common for Christians to wait until they have had a crisis before they open the Bible. Let's say a person loses their job, home and children all in the same week. If that person is not familiar with God's true nature of grace and mercy, they may open to the book of Job and begin to form an incorrect view of God. It may not be possible to be 100 percent prepared before we face a given event, but the more proper view we have of the Bible and the true nature of God, the better off we will be when hard times come. It is obviously much better to know as much as possible about the Bible and the true nature of our Heavenly Father before we experience difficult times. Then, we will already know how to deal with different

81

situations. We will also know why they are happening, or at least know that it is not God punishing us for something Jesus has already paid for through His stripes and sacrifice.

For instance, **John 10:10** tells us that we have an enemy who has come to steal, kill and destroy. The enemy is of course the Devil. Some believe that God has Satan on a leash and will choose what he can and cannot do in our lives. We have already established that man is the one who allows Satan to have his way in our lives in an earlier chapter. That small amount of knowledge can make all the difference when hard times come.

When we have a wrong view of God, it will affect our ability to receive from Him. I personally am not afraid to tell others to go back to the Word of God on their own and research what I tell them. I have said this many times in front of large crowds when I speak in churches and other ministry settings. Most ministers and or pastors would be horrified at doing such a thing. There are numerous reasons why I do this. One of the main goals is to provide an opportunity for others to allow God to give them their own revelation of His Word. When we trust God to reveal truth to us, it will quickly revolutionize our walk with Him.

In many church settings, it is not uncommon to hear a message that ties God's love and willingness to bless us solely to our own individual performance and then tied to our "prayer closet" time, tithing, obedience, etc. This way of thinking is not only unbiblical, but as we have seen with Job's three friends, it is not a new way of thinking by any means. In **Job 8:6,** Bildad essentially tells Job that God would be good to him if he were being good to God.

This is exactly what I am talking about; many tie any problem we have in life to God's direct love for us, or lack of love for us. Bildad accused Job of being a wicked man. Just as with the barnyard example that I used earlier, we are going to have to deal with the result of things that have fallen. Nevertheless, that does not mean it is the desire of God for things to take place that way, no more than a dairy farmer wants us to step in cow patties while visiting his farm.

In **Job 8:7,** Bildad reacts to Job's belief that nothing good will ever happen to him again and ties what *will* happen to Job to his performance, once again.

Bildad was on the right track when he told Job that God still had good things in store for him. However, he was wrong to tell Job that he must repent in order for God to bless him again. I am not saying that we should not repent of any sin in our lives but we must understand that it is not our performance but rather the performance of Jesus that makes the difference for us under the New Covenant.

On a side note, let's discuss repentance for a short time. I believe that many Christians do not properly understand the difference between receiving forgiveness of our sins and repenting of our sins.

Plainly put, forgiveness is God's part. He provided forgiveness for all sin, one time, through the cross **(2 Corinthians 5:19-21, 1 John 2:2)**. God has forgiven us of all sin: past, present, and future. Nevertheless, we must receive that forgiveness by becoming born again in order for it to operate in our lives. Just because we receive that forgiveness does not mean we have repented of our sins.

The word repent is defined as meaning, "changing of one's mind" **(Romans 12:1-2)**.

84

The process of repenting means that we renew our mind and change our habits and or behavior patterns so that sin will cease in our lives. Garbage in does *not* equal Gospel out. In some cases, we may need to distance ourselves with those who are not a Godly influence in our lives. In making changes as to what we allow into our minds we will in turn change the way we act and how we live. By first "changing our minds", the way we believe about a certain thing, we will have established the necessary foundation to "turn from" sin.

In some cases, the problem of sin can come from within the four walls of the church. Again, this may come as a shock, but notice that often we don't see the level of strife in relationships outside of the church as we see in relationships within the church.

Anything that produces doubt and unbelief is not from or of God. I know this is not the common way of thinking but if you don't want common results, you must walk an uncommon road.

I could write a completely new book on this topic and in time that may happen. I would like to go much further in discussing this but to save time and space I am not going to do so. If you would like to know more about the differences between forgiveness and repentance, I urge you to research the Bible.

The interesting thing about the book of Job is that throughout it we see so much of what is taking place in the modern day church and so-called Christianity. Much of what Job's friends told him is exactly what we hear today. This might explain why the book of Job is cited so often when bad things happen.

Many of the following chapters in the book of Job obtain more of this sort of information. We can see many more examples of Job being misled by his friends. Of course, there are also some areas in which these friends give Job some accurate and helpful information. However, for the most part, they are all pointing their finger at God as the ultimate source for Job's problems.

In Job chapter 10, Job continues to rant, and is complaining in much the same manner as what we have all done at some point or another. I wish I could say I am exempt from this but I am not. When I stop and think about the times I have complained, I can say with confidence, complaining has done me no good.

Job now throws caution to the wind and speaks out of anger and frustration. He knows what he is doing but does not care, as of **Job 10:1**. In fact, this is the case throughout all of chapter 10.

Chapter 9

Zophar Speaks Up
———— W ————

Now the last of the group of Job's three friends, Zophar, speaks. He also speaks up in chapter 11 and chapter 20. Just as is the case with Eliphaz and Bildad, what Zophar has to say is not meant to be taken as scriptural fact. If you remember what we discussed in chapter 2, this should not come as a surprise to you. We can read the book of Job and say it is true that Job's friends told him his problems came via the judgment of God. Nevertheless, before you finish reading this book, I hope you will be able to see the truth clearly that God was not the reason for Job's problems at all. We have already begun to establish this point and will continue to do so as we move forward.

Zophar was in the right to recognize that Job was being self-centered in his actions. It was all about Job! We have all fallen into this trap at one time or another. I am not trying to make light of any difficult times you may have dealt with. However, it never really makes us feel any better when we only focus inwardly, rather than on others who have also been affected by what has made us sad. Let's begin reviewing what Zophar had to say with **Job 11:3-4**.

Zophar heads down the same road as did Eliphaz and Bildad. While he did recognize the problem with Job's selfishness, he also believed that Job was a terrible sinner and that his experiences were a direct result of sin in his life. Again, many in the modern day church take this very path not only because of what they have read in the book of Job, but because it simply makes sense to our five senses that bad things can come because of God's correction in our lives. Nevertheless, let's not forget **2 Timothy 3:16**. God disciplines us through his Word (the Bible), not through natural circumstances!

Many may say, "what about Romans 8:28?" as they quote by saying, "all things work together for good". Let's take a quick look at this verse to help clear up the confusion.

It may be safe to say that **Romans 8:28** is the most well known verse in the entire Bible. It is not uncommon to hear non-believers quote this verse. It is obviously more common to hear it from Christians but most fail to use the entire verse and if they do so, they are usually not properly using its context.

In times of bad circumstances, many will utter, *"All things work together for good"*. Did you know that this is not what **Romans 8:28** says*?* **Romans 8:28** actually says, ***"And we know that all things work together for good to them that love God, to them who are the called according to his purpose"*.** If it were true that all things work together for good, then it would not matter if a person were born again or not. All things would work together for good in every person's life. This is simply not so*!*

The first thing we need to do is focus on the very first word found in **Romans 8:28**: the word "And". That tells us that what we are reading needs to be tied into the previous verse. If we simply read **Romans 8:28** by itself it will be very easy to misuse the verse and this is exactly what happens on a regular basis. If you remember, I earlier made a point of not waiting to have a crisis or any experience before we open the Bible. We need to filter our experiences through the Bible, rather than filtering our "beliefs about God's Word" through our experiences. By following this simple principle, we will have a better chance of not forming bad and incorrect doctrine. One of the best methods for doing this is to pay close attention to the first word of verses such as **Romans 8:28** which begins with the conjunction "And". This means everything being said in verse 28 is dependent on what was said in verse 27.

Romans 8:27, "And he that searcheth the hearts knoweth what is the mind of the Spirit, because he maketh intercession for the saints according to the will of God".

Romans 8:27 is speaking of the Holy spirit making intercessions with us. In order for this to happen, we must cooperate. The Holy Spirit does not work in our lives unless we allow. Many believe that the Holy Spirit just takes over and we all of a sudden, have no control over what we do. This is also untrue and against what the Bible teaches.

1 Corinthians 14:32 - And the spirits of the prophets are subject to the prophets.

This is simply saying that "the spirits" are under our control. If a person who is baptized in the Holy Spirit wants to pray in tongues, they can start and stop as they wish.

Another important point to notice concerning **Romans 8:28** is that the verse does not say that all things come from God. The way most are using the verse gives the impression that all things are from and of God, but this line of thinking simply is not accurate according to the scriptures.

In reality, **Romans 8:28** is speaking of what can happen when we are interceding in the spirit. We can take anything the Devil throws in our direction and turn it around for good. That makes a huge difference in how the verse reads. However, if we misuse the verse to make it say that all things come from God, we are opening the door to the Devil. This works against us, because we are likely to yield to anything we believe is from or of God and not resist what we believe is coming from the enemy. Satan will then be able to run us over with a steamroller, put the machine in reverse and run over us in the opposite direction, and repeat the process all day long. This answers a question as to why some people are constantly dealing with one problem or another. They are the very ones who tend to say, "God is in control" on a regular basis.

Remember, we seldom hear that phrase until something bad has happened. When we return to Job chapter 11, we see Zophar claiming that his words toward Job are right and accurate.

In **Job 11:4**, Zophar was standing in the same shoes as many Christians do today. I have heard well-meaning Christians give inaccurate information to others who are in need of encouragement. They may tell a mother who just lost their child in a car accident, that it was God who allowed it to happen. They may say that God needed that child in Heaven, more than his family on Earth needed him. Of course, nothing could be further from the truth. While a person who gives such information may be speaking from a pure and well-meaning heart, that does not mean they are operating out of a pure and correct knowledge. That is exactly what Zophar was doing, as well as Job's other two friends. They meant well but that does not automatically make them right in what they were saying to Job.

Job and Zophar both longed for God to show up and give an answer as to why the events in Job's life had taken place. This is where things begin to get interesting.

What Zophar said in **Job 11:7** is where we get the phrase "God's ways are higher than our ways". **Isaiah 55:9** says *"For as the heavens are higher than the Earth, so are my ways higher than your ways, and my thoughts than your thoughts."* This simply means that God thinks differently than sinful man. Many people will say, *"You never know what God is going to do"*. However, God has revealed his thoughts and plans to us through the Holy Spirit **(1 Corinthians 2:9-15)**.

Zophar was correct in making this statement. However, Zophar also told Job that he was wrong to criticize God, but again, Zophar was in the wrong to condemn Job at all. While Eliphaz, Bildad, and Zophar did not condemn God, they did accuse and condemn Job. They were wrong to do so as it was not God or Job's fault that the terrible events had taken place. Let's not forget that none of these men had a revelation of the Devil. If the name "Satan" had been mentioned to any of them they probably would have responded with, "Who?"

Zophar continues to condemn Job for what he believes is hidden sin in Job's life. If you have ever had a person do this to you then you know the condemnation and guilt that flows out of such thinking. Zophar also proclaims Job arrogant and compares him to a donkey.

Over the course of the next several chapters, you will find much more of the same dialog that we have already looked into. Job continues in a downward spiral of self-centeredness, while his friends continue to condemn him.

The same events are still taking place today both inside and outside of the four walls of the Church. We have more flesh than spirit so it is very easy to fall into the trap of trying to find reasons for difficult circumstances that fit what our five senses can understand. Nevertheless, that does not mean the typical viewpoint of why bad things happen, is correct.

How often have we been in a setting when terrible tragedies, such as the death of those close to us or the relative of those close to us, have taken place? It could involve a divorce, the loss of a job, a natural disaster, and many other areas of suffering. We often hear **Job 1:21** quoted at funerals and during times of tragedy of different types. The book of Job continues to be misused as a cornerstone to explain why bad events take place.

However, outside of the book of Job, there is what I like to call a Christian buzzword that is commonly uttered more than any other in the most difficult of circumstances. The word I am referring to is the word *"sovereign"*.

Chapter 10

The Sovereignty of God

In chapters 1 and 2 of this book, I used the illustration of a job I held several years ago, looking for dents and imperfections in automobiles. The illustration was given, to show the importance of changing our viewpoint. As we gain a completely different perspective, we see things from a different angle, and find things that we would not have seen otherwise. We also stressed the importance of separating what is true from what is *truth*. These are very important concepts to keep in mind as we begin to look at the word "sovereign".

The word "sovereign" has become a popular and commonly used word in the church today. Just as is the case with the phrase "God is in control", we seldom, if ever, hear the word "sovereign" until something bad has happened. Nevertheless, I have a question for you; have you ever looked up this "Christian buzzword" in the dictionary to discover its true meaning? Just in case you have not, I have provided the dictionary.com definition below.

Sovereign - One that exercises authority in a limited sphere. 2. An acknowledged leader. 3. independent. 4. Excellent.

I once watched a video on the Internet in which a pastor spoke about sovereignty. He gave a definition very similar to what you just read but he also gave some additional insight. He said, "But I like to say the word sovereign means "God is in control".

Essentially, what this pastor was saying is that he would rather use the definition created by religion, as opposed to what the dictionary really says concerning the word sovereign or sovereignty. As you can see, the word sovereign, does *not* mean "in control of" everything that happens. Nevertheless, this is what the modern day church has presented. There are even denominations that believe God controls every little thing that happens. They believe God is in the smallest of details. However, I have yet to meet anyone who says, "God is in control of everything that happens", who actually believes this one hundred percent.

They always draw the line at a place of personal convenience.

In reality, the word sovereign does define God perfectly, in its proper meaning. He is at the top of the food chain, so-to-speak, (is an acknowledged leader) and does not take orders from anybody (is independent). Nevertheless, this does not mean that God "controls" everything that takes place on the Earth.

Earlier we looked at Genesis chapter 1, in which God gave man "control" over everything on the Earth and in the Earth. *That is very important to remember!* Why do you think the Earth is in such terrible shape today? It surely isn't because God wanted it to be that way. It is due primarily, to the poor decisions being made by mankind, and we all have a part to play in that area. One of the leading reasons in the popularity of the common "Sovereignty of God" belief system is that it excuses us from most if not all responsibility when things don't go the "right" way.

So, where did the word sovereign gain its popularity? Has it always been a word used since the foundations of the world? The answer is, no. Let's take a further look into the misuse of this word.

The New International Version of the Bible uses the word "sovereign" more than any other version of the Bible. It is used 303 times in the Old Testament alone but is not found anywhere in the King James. In the NIV, *sovereign* always appears along with Lord (Sovereign Lord) and is equivalent to the King James Version of "Lord God". Here is an example:

Genesis 15:2, And Abram said, *LORD God*, what wilt thou give me, seeing I go childless, and the steward of my house is this Eliezer of Damascus? (KJV)

Genesis 15:2, But Abram said, "O *Sovereign LORD*, what can you give me since I remain childless and the one who will inherit my estate is Eliezer of Damascus?" (NIV)

The example seen in **Genesis 15:2** illustrates my point quite well.

Another interesting area to consider is that none of the verses in which you see "Lord God" or "Sovereign Lord" has anything to do with control! I know this may come as a tremendous shock to you and may even go as far as to offend some people. In our modern day, both inside and outside of the church, it has been taught that we should shun responsibility for the most part. Let's face it, it's much easier to blame others when things don't work out as opposed to just saying, "I made a mistake". The Bible is very clear about the fact that our own decisions determine how things will go for us. **Proverbs 19:3** is the perfect example to use in this matter.

"The foolishness of man perverteth his way: and his heart fretteth against the LORD." (KJV)

However, I believe the Message translation of the Bible puts it far better in this case.

Proverbs 19:3, "People ruin their lives by their own stupidity, so why does God always get blamed?" (MESSAGE TRANSLATION)

Let's face it! It is always much easier to blame others, and even God, when things don't work out for us. It makes us feel better for a short time, but we all can admit that the short-lived comfort produced from this form of thinking is not something that is long lasting.

However, if God does control everything that happens on the Earth, then it is the logical conclusion everything happens because God wants it to. As I have already mentioned, there are some denominations who call themselves Christians that actually believe God controls every single event that takes place: PERIOD*!* If this is so, then it means that God's will always happens no matter what the case may be. However, the Bible reveals the truth concerning what God's will truly is when we read **2 Peter 3:9**.

"The Lord is not slack concerning his promise, as some men count slackness; but is longsuffering to us-ward, not willing that any should perish, but that all should come to repentance."

We have already discussed the word, repent, in an earlier chapter. We know that it means, *"Changing of one's mind"*. In the simplest terms, **2 Peter 3:9** is saying that it is God's will that *everybody* become born again and that nobody spends eternity in hell. However, there are simply too many people that are not accepting the truth of the Gospel for this to be accomplished. Nevertheless, the Bible says that it is God's will that nobody spends eternity in hell. Therefore, we can conclude that the will of God does not automatically come to pass.

Jesus Himself said that many more would perish than those who would come to repentance **(Matthew 7:13)**. The Scriptures clearly declare that it is God's will for every single person who walks the Earth to become born again. Remember, Jesus didn't die for our sins only but for the sins of the whole world, **(1 John 2:2)**. I know that there will be many people who will call what I am saying "blasphemy", but I choose to allow the Bible to determine what I believe in this matter and all others.

Let's face it, we all hate to look bad and have to admit that we missed it. It is always much easier to just take what we may not understand and throw responsibility on God. I'll use praying for the sick to be healed as an example.

If you study the Bible in the area of healing, it is simple to see that it is always God's will to heal. It is also always God's will for everyone to be born again but as we already know, that is not happening. God's will does not just automatically happen. Many people have prayed and believed for healing, whether it is for themselves or for someone else, but have not always seen the manifestation of that healing take place. Unfortunately, it is very easy to begin to wonder why our prayers are not being answered. If we believe that God is the one who controls who is healed and who is not, we instantly begin to form an unbiblical view and doctrine concerning God and His plan for healing. Nevertheless, it's convenient and makes for a great excuse when needed!

Some people are quick to let you know that they were the ones who prayed for someone who was healed of cancer. However, if that person was to die of cancer, or anything else for that matter, most Christians would simply say, "We don't know why *God allowed* them to die, but praise God, He's in control". It is much easier to shove the blame over onto God then to say *we* are the one who missed something. We need to be spiritually mature and remember that God is not the problem at any point, and accept our responsibility *without* allowing ourselves to fall under any form of condemnation.

Acts 10:38 tells us that Jesus went about doing "good" and "healing all because God was with Him". Jesus never told a single person that it was not His Father's will for them to be healed. We can draw a very simple, yet profound conclusion from what Jesus said and did as He taught His disciples concerning this topic. **Hebrews 13:8** tells us that Jesus Christ is the same yesterday, today, and forever. In **John 5:19** Jesus said that He only did what He saw the father (God) do. If we tie **John 5:19**, **Acts 10:38**, and **Hebrews 13:8** together, it is not hard at all to see that it is always God's will to heal. So why do we not see every person healed? I cannot necessarily answer that question for every case but I can say one thing for sure. *The problem is never on God's end!* The bottom line is that we cannot draw the conclusion when someone dies that it was just God's plan. That *may* bring temporary relief or it may just throw gasoline on the fire and turn that dear one against God. In either case, this is not only an answer that fails to bring any sort of satisfaction, but it is also not a Biblically based answer.

As I have already said, I know this is not a popular belief among the majority of professing Christians, but when did following the majority become the best thing to do? Just consider **Matthew 7:13-14** in this matter. The majority will always take the easy road.

I firmly do *not* believe that God controls everything that happens. I believe that He "independently" made the decision to put man in control of the Earth. You may agree that the word "sovereign" does not mean "in control of" everything that happens. However, what happens when we have been doing our best to believe in faith for a long time and we seemingly are not getting the desired results? It is tempting to get out of faith and begin to walk *after* the flesh. At this point we can get mad at God and ask Him why He isn't moving on our behalf, and in doing so, we have negated our faith and shoved the answer to our prayer even further away. It's a simple reality: Living in faith is much harder to accomplish than is living by flesh and out of the understanding our five senses.

If we allow what we feel, hear, touch, taste, smell, and see to determine if we believe God has done His part or not, we are in for a long and miserable ride. That's just the way it is.

The wrong view of the sovereignty of God will produce passivity and that is exactly what Satan wants from us! If he can convince us that things are not working out because God doesn't want them to, then we have no reason to do anything but just learn to live with the problem. Whether it be sickness and financial lack, relationship turmoil, or in bondage to a habit, depression, a drug, or any other form of bondage, we are not going to get anywhere if we just believe that everything will take place in what the Church has labeled "God's timing". If things are not working out, we need to seek God and ask Him what we need to do differently. For example, if you are a business owner who sells a particular product, you may need to pray for your customer's finances. If they are not blessed, they will not have the necessary finances to purchase your products. They must be in a position to have a need for your product and be able to afford it in order for your business to succeed. If those things do not come together then your business will not be successful. Nevertheless, that does not mean your business will fail because God wanted it to. God is not making choices about what does and does not go on in our lives. We are the ones who are making those choices, *not* God. As hard as it may be to accept, that's just the way it is.

If I want to know a person's belief system I will ask them one simple question; "Does Satan have to go to God to get permission for anything he does?" Most people will answer "yes" and cite the book of Job in doing so. However, as we have already seen, God didn't give Satan power over the Earth. Rather, it was mankind who relinquished his God given authority and power over the Earth to Satan that ultimately allowed the enemy to do what he did to Job.

The most dangerous part of the wrong view of the sovereignty of God is how it flings the door open to Satan in our lives. He can steal from us without us even knowing what is going on. If we truly believe something is from or of God, we would be in outright rebellion against Him to resist whatever has come our way. This is one of the biggest reasons, why it is so dangerous to believe that God controls everything.

Before we reach the end of this book, you will see God defend Himself and clearly tell Job and his friends that He was *not* the one who caused or allowed Job's problems. A lot of what I will be revealing in coming pages will be the information you will not hear in the vast majority of churches. Nevertheless, it is the *truth!* Please allow me to close this chapter with one last but very important point.

If you go to your concordance and search for the word "sovereign", you may be in for a surprise. That surprise will be that the word "sovereign", is not found in the concordance. This is just something else for you to consider!

Chapter 11

Satan is _Not_ God's Messenger Boy

In my opinion, one of the absolute worst prayers a person can pray is, "Lord, whatever it takes". This may sound like a wonderful prayer to our flesh but in reality, it flings to door open to the Devil.

When I was in Bible College, I spent some time working a job in which I met some very interesting people. Some of these people were just as nice and polite as they could be. They were very respectful, and wouldn't pitch a fit if they disagreed with something I believed or said. There was one man who was a Calvinist and while he was very proud of his beliefs, he didn't try to force his beliefs on others. There was also a man who seemed like a super nice person and when all was said and done, he really _was_ just what he appeared to be. During one of my first few days on the job, the man I referred to as being "super nice" began to talk to me about different things concerning the Bible.

After the conversation, I felt as if this man really knew the truth about God and God's true nature. Boy was I ever wrong!

The next night, I was walking in one direction and saw this man, who we'll call John, coming from the other direction. We started to chat and he told me that he had a great song he wanted me to listen to on his CD player. I said okay and put the earphones on. The song "Blessed be your name" began to play. I listened for a few seconds and then removed the earphones. I told John that I had heard the song many times before but didn't like it. I went on to explain that the reason for my dislike of the song had to do with the bridge. The bridge I am referring to contains the words "You give and take away".

We have already looked at the fact that Job did indeed utter the words, "The Lord gives and the Lord takes away" in **Job 1:21**. We have also looked at the fact that Job may have said those words, but it was not God who took anything from Job. Many people sing the song I am referring to and breeze right through the bridge without giving it a second thought. The wrong view of **Job 1:21** gives God a black eye for many terrible events that He did not cause or allow, yet we sing about Him as if He is the one to blame when bad things happen. While some of the words to *'Blessed be your Name'* may be good, I refuse to sing the words written in the bridge. I simply change them to, "You give to me each day"*!*

Some even say, "I choose to look at **Job 1:21** in the light that God gives good things to set us free and takes away the bondages that entangle us". This is a great way to look at this particular scripture. However, in reality, it is not what Job meant when he uttered those misused words, nor is it what most folks mean when they sing those words.

After I explained to John why I didn't like the song, an interesting conversation began. A good friend of mine often speaks of a message he heard many years ago that was titled, "Satan is God's messenger boy". That particular message produced sickness and death in his friend, and it was not a message from or of God, but rather of the Devil. It's a long story that I don't have time to get into right now. However, the reason I bring this up is that John told me the very same thing, "Satan is God's messenger boy*!*" It made me think back to the story my other friend related to me. John went on to tell the story that was just plain wrong. It was so far outside the truth of how God actually relates to us, that it amazed me! His story was meant to illustrate that God did indeed use Satan as his messenger boy in order to accomplish His will.

John's story had to do with a man who was a pastor. This pastor had a daughter who was away from God and headed down a wrong road. I don't even think she was born again, but I don't remember for sure. Either way, she was not serving God and had become involved in a lifestyle in which she had no business. One day he prayed for her and during his prayer, he said "Lord, whatever it takes". He was praying for his daughter to get away from all of the ungodliness in her life and turn to God. Not long after praying this prayer, the pastor was involved in a car accident. It was not a major accident as his car had been rear ended by another vehicle. He was sore but otherwise okay. After getting out of the car, the pastor began to talk to the person who had rear-ended his vehicle. He had been out of his car and walking around for several minutes when he suddenly fell to the ground. This pastor had blacked-out, and was taken to the hospital. He ended up being in a coma for a long while and things did not look good at all. Time passed by and there was no improvement.

As is common, his family began to struggle with fear and worry concerning what the possible outcome of the situation may be. During this long period, the pastor's daughter turned her life around, stopped living a life of sin, and turned to God. She did so in part, due to the situation that had taken place with her father. Not long after this great event had transpired, the pastor began to improve and in time made a full recovery.

It was said that by him praying, "Lord, whatever it takes", that the prayer had made the difference. Many believed that it was God who had orchestrated all of the events that had taken place.

This may sound like an amazing testimony, and it is not uncommon to hear it both inside and outside the church today. A great many people believe this. However, it is completely unbiblical. God was not the reason for the events that took place by a long shot. In fact, the door was opened to the Devil when he prayed, "whatever it takes" for his daughter to get her life right.

You may be saying, why would this pastor's prayer have been what caused everything to take place as it did? It's plain and simple! God doesn't put problems or tragedies in our lives to make us turn to Him.

We have already looked at the importance of living in faith and not out of our five senses. If we live out of our five senses, we will look for explanations to difficult circumstances that make sense based on what we can feel, hear, see, smell, and taste. There is no faith involved in such a case. It is not a good idea to wait until we have had a negative experience before we go to the Bible. However, this is quite common today. Many people do not study and research the Bible until something difficult has taken place in their lives. They will then go to the Bible, to try to find an event in scripture that matches what they are experiencing. This methodology will produce bad doctrine on a regular basis.

The problem with the particular prayer I am speaking about is that it opened the door to the Devil. In essence what we are saying when we pray, "Lord, whatever it takes", is that we don't care if it takes cancer, a life altering car wreck, or even death; we want anything it takes in order for our particular prayer to be answered. In the case of the pastor I have been using as an illustration, it was his desire to see his daughters life changed for the better. His heart may have been in the right place by praying such a prayer, but his knowledge **(Hosea 4:6)** of how to pray to that end, was far from accurate. When we pray this same type of prayer, we are letting our guard down. We are removing all protection that keeps Satan's attacks from being successful in our lives. Never forget, he only wants to steal, kill and destroy **(John 10:10)**.

We have already established the point that Satan does not need God's permission to do anything at all. The book of Job is an absolute favorite among those who believe he does. This is why I believe the events that took place in that pastor's life went down as they did. He had let his guard down, and he was willing to take on any bad situation if it would lead to his daughter getting her life back on the right track. It might make sense to our physical being, our five senses, and in our "own understanding", to pray the same way in such a situation. However, that is completely against everything that the Bible teaches.

Many people don't see a need to trust God until things get really bad. When they are at the end of their rope, then they turn to God as their last resort. It's really a sad issue on many fronts. It shows the lack of properly presenting God as anything more than just a failsafe. This is the fault of the modern day church, and what they call discipleship! God is typically presented as a "get out of hell free" card. Obviously, salvation covers keeping us out of hell, but there is so much more. We have already seen that God sent a sacrifice in our place to pay for all sin. The only way to miss Heaven is not to accept that sacrifice (Jesus). In reality, *the primary purpose of salvation is to be able to have relationship with God.* Sadly, this is something that is rarely heard in many traditional and even 'modernized' church settings. In fact, many professing Christians, wait until something difficult happens before they call on their relationship with God. It's as if we have been taught to believe, that our relationship with God is only formed during difficult times. I don't believe that this is how it was modeled for us by Jesus, or designed to work in the first place.

If we wait until difficult times before we search the scriptures, as we have already pointed out, we are more likely to form incorrect doctrine. The same thing applies to relationship with God and even other people. *Relationship is not formed in difficult times but rather sustains us in difficult times!*

There is so much wrong with believing everything happens because God wants it to. I recently heard a pastor who spoke of how God will often lead us into difficult times. He used **Jeremiah 27, 28, and 29** as his text. In doing so, he compared us to the Israelites. While we can learn from what happened to the Israelites, there are some key differences between them and us. They could not be born again. Again, this may come as a shock but let's step back and think for a minute. What Savior did the Israelites have? Jesus had not yet come which means nobody could be born again. In fact, there is nobody in the Old Testament who was born again.

Another key difference between the Israelites and us today is that they also did not have the Holy Spirit to lead and guide them. When God sent His Spirit, mankind gained the ability to know things he could not know as easily as before. According to **John 14:26**, the Spirit will reveal to us all things and bring all things to our remembrance.

John 14:26, "But the Comforter, which is the Holy Ghost, whom the Father will send in my name, he shall teach you all things, and bring all things to your remembrance, whatsoever I have said unto you."

This is an important area to consider. Job also was not born again, and therefore did not have the Holy Spirit to reveal to him all things and bring all things to his remembrance.

If God leads us into difficult times and thus controls everything that happens, we have no business ever resisting anything that is from or of God. This is a trap that Satan wants us to fall into. If we believe a thing is from or of God, then we are more likely to bow down to it. Let's look at the book of James in order to solidify this point.

James 4:7 - Submit yourselves therefore to God. Resist the Devil, and he will flee from you.

If everything that happens in our lives happens because God wants it to, then that means God works through Satan in some, if not all instances. This is where the belief that Satan is God's messenger boy comes from. So what happens if God is the one who chooses what Satan can and cannot do? It means that we should never resist Satan if he is being used to fulfill God's will in some way, shape, or form. If God works through Satan, we should not resist the Devil because that would mean we are in turn resisting God.

This is a horrible trap that Satan would love for us to fall into. If we believe that God leads us into problems, whether it is through Satan or not, it opens a wide open door for the Devil to steal from us. He will be able to do so without any resistance because we have allowed ourselves to become passive and are not resisting him at all. He can come into our life with a steamroller and run right over us. If we have the wrong understanding in this area, he can then put the steamroller in reverse and run right over us repeatedly, and we will never resist!

It is so important that we gain a different viewpoint, in order to see what is plainly in the

Scriptures concerning these areas that affect every one of us. However, if we dig in our heels and proclaim, "I've never heard that before, I don't believe it", then we will continue to miss the *truth* that has been right in front of us all along. I am not suggesting that you can get to a point of living a problem free life, but the correct way of thinking concerning why the Devil can do what he does will go a long way in seeing vast improvements in every area of your life.

Chapter 12

There is Nothing New Under the Sun
———— W ————

Ecclesiastes 1:9 - The thing that hath been, it is that which shall be; and that which is done is that which shall be done: and there is no new thing under the sun.

There is nothing taking place today that has not already taken place at some point in the past. Anger and strife are something we see throughout all of history. Murder was first committed long ago during the time of Cain and Able. The religious traditionalists have always stood in the way of enjoying a relaxed relationship with God as opposed to keeping every custom. People have also been blaming God for things that were absolutely not from or of Him. *"There is no new thing under the sun."*

Proverbs 19:3, People ruin their lives by their own stupidity, so why does GOD always get blamed? (Message Bible)

It is obvious that people have been blaming God for bad things for a very long time. This is exactly what we have seen taking place throughout the book of Job. God must have thick skin to put up with the accusations He deals with on a regular basis. I have to admit that I don't think I would continue to give the same mercy and grace that God gives if I was accused of sending hurricanes, causing a person to lose their job or killing their loved ones. Gratefully, I'm not God so it will never be a problem! These are just a few examples of what God has had thrown in His direction on a regular basis. Nevertheless, **GOD IS NOT GUILTY**! We need to remember that it is the thief that has come to steal, kill, and destroy **(John 10:10)**. That thief of course is Satan and he is not God's messenger boy! God does not have Satan on a leash that only allows him to do so much. According to **Proverbs 19:3**, our own decisions and choices allow Satan to have his way. I know this isn't the popular thing to say but neither were the messages presented by

Jesus and Paul, and look at what they had to deal with while walking the Earth!

Each time I read through the book of Job, I always see things that are still being done today. Many today are still blaming God for bad things and trying to come up with a justifiable reason why God would allow terrible events to take place. There are even multitudes of people who take the same road as Eliphaz, Bildad, and Zophar. They believe that a person's problems and even their own tragic circumstances are due to the judgment of God. Let's not forget that Jesus was judged in our place and there is now no reason for us to be judged a second time.

Romans 8:1 - There is therefore now no condemnation to them which are in Christ Jesus, who walk not after the flesh, but after the Spirit.

If a person is born again, there is absolutely no condemnation for them. It seems as if many in the church today never "got the memo". Many will turn to the book of Job and cite the words of Job's friends to back up their belief that God is sending pain and suffering to judge not only individuals but also entire nations.

This is simply wrong! However, there remain many instances in the book of Job in which we hear words that are still being uttered today. Job was deeply involved in self-pity throughout most of the book of Job. It truly reminds me of events we see in the lives of people today, when they have become self centered.

Don't get me wrong. I am not trying to make light of any difficult situation that anyone may face. I know many of you who are reading this book have faced things far worse than anything I have ever dealt with. However, allowing our five senses to rein and rule over our emotions, only serves to compound the issues. This is the world's way of dealing with difficult circumstances and even tragedy. However, just because we live in a fallen world does not mean we have to act like the fallen world. Remember, we have God's Word, which is full of so many powerful and positive promises. Please don't ever make the mistake of thinking you are Job.

I once had a friend who told me that he was Job. He was in the midst of a very difficult time in his life. His business was on the brink of closing, he was having marital problems and he was about to be forced to sell a very nice home. He was focused on himself but not on others.

128

He wound up paying a price for his wrong way of thinking. He reacted in fear to his circumstances, which opened the door to the Devil. I can promise you, the Devil was 'revving the engine' on his steamroller just waiting for an opportunity. Had my friend responded in faith, no matter how hard it may have been, the outcome most assuredly, would have been better. I cannot say what the differences might have been, but they surely would have been better than responding in fear. When we turn to God in faith, it's like throwing a monkey wrench into the Devils steamroller that stops it from running! Sadly, my friend did not do so and wound up losing everything he feared losing, including his marriage. Trust me, that was never God's plan for his life from the beginning. Nevertheless, it was much easier for him to blame God than to look in the mirror and say, "what in me needs to change?"

I know it's hard for us to admit that we are the problem. However, we will find a "fix" for our situation much sooner when we do so. Remember, even if we did not put ourselves in a tough spot, we are the ones who choose how we will react to the given situation. This is a very important point that we all need to hear repeatedly.

Obviously, we can read the book of Job and see many instances in which the actions of those such as Job and his friends are not much different from what we see today. Sure, they did not have the wide range of ways to vent and let others know how they feel as we have today. Nevertheless, had they had the Internet and all of the social networking websites, you can count on the fact that many people would have been reading about their feelings concerning the situation. I wonder if anyone would have had the guts to stand up to them and say, "Who do you think you are to blame God for these events?"

In chapter 13, Job begins to reprove his friends and claim they are partial.

Job 13:1 - Lo, mine eye hath seen all this, mine ear hath heard and understood it.

Job was in essence saying that he knew God would punish sin but he also knew that his problem did not stem from sin. Job was absolutely correct in all he had just said. His three friends had really begun to frustrate him as they had been talking down to him as if he knew nothing. It was just not the right time to be doing so. Even if all of what the three friends had spoken had been accurate, they were still very much out of line in kicking their friend while he was down. Let's face it, sometimes people try to come to our aid but end up doing more harm than good. I believe Job's friends were not the right people to come to Job's aid, but they did and caused a lot more trouble than Job bargained for.

Have you ever done something that you knew was wrong but went ahead and did it anyway? I think we all have. Some of us may have done so on a larger scale than others, but this is something I believe we can all identify with. Job could also identify with doing what he knew was wrong to do.

Earlier in the book of Job, **(Job 9:14)** he had said he would not reason with God as he knew this was the wrong thing to do. However, in **Job 13:3** he changed his mind and wanted to do what he knew was wrong.

Job 13:3, Surely I would speak to the Almighty, and I desire to reason with God.

Over the course of the next few verses we see Job's anger towards his friends rise at a fast pace. In **13:5** he tells his friends to stop speaking, which would in turn make them look much wiser than they were making themselves look at this point.

I know there is a lot more that I could hit on in Job 13, as well as other chapters, but I want to encourage you to spend some time researching for yourself. I am now going to hit on some important points concerning the fact that there is *'nothing new under the sun'*. This is seen in many more instances throughout the remaining chapters in Job.

Job 14:1, Man that is born of a woman is of few days, and full of trouble.

Job 14:1 is a very relevant scripture to appear in this chapter. In this particular scripture, Job was making a point that all of mankind has problems. He was saying that we don't live as long as we may wish to and we all face many challenges and struggles. Job was correct in saying this and it lines right up with living in a fallen world. An interesting side note concerns the fact that Job lived roughly 200 years and possibly a little longer. Can you imagine what he would think if he was alive today?

As I have said, God must be thick skinned to put up with so many false accusations being thrown in His direction. Some of us can cite a time when we have questioned why God ever bothered to give us the breath of life. When we allow ourselves to become focused on self, it can quickly cause us to become blind in many areas. Remember, it's not all about us! Nevertheless, He did it all *for* us*!*

Job was determined to deem himself as being insignificant. He wanted to know why God would even notice him and why God would allow and/or cause such difficulties in his life. This is something we have all heard others say and may have even asked ourselves. Job was angry with God because he felt that God was the ultimate one who chose to cause the events that took place in his life. **Job 14:3** is an example of how many Christians believe today. In fact, it isn't just Christians who believe that God is at the root of all bad things.

Before my Mom ever became a born again believer, she would often wonder why God did bad things to her. She once told me about how she would wonder what she had done wrong that God would make her to stub her toe! In her own words she told me, "I would ask, what have I done wrong now for God to have made me stub my toe?" That is amazing! Nevertheless, I believe the ultimate reason that non-believers will blame God for tragedies, has to do with the modern day views of God portrayed by the Church. In reality, the church is not doing a very good job, (for the most part) of representing God. Many are in deep division and strife. Christians seem to be the only ones who are willing to 'shoot their wounded' as the saying goes. Instead of doing what we saw Jesus do in the Bible, when it comes to dealing with sin in a person's life, the church will say, "repent! Turn or burn! Get right with God or you're going to hell!" The "death, hell, and the grave" message has chased away many people.

I remember a particular situation that my Mom witnessed that may shock some people. You would think we would be safe from prejudice inside the four walls of the Church. However, in many cases, the inside of a church offers no more hope and love than the world does. This story really surprised me.

A now well-known evangelist had come to speak at the church we were attending at the time. He had been several times before and was beginning to become well-known. It was a pleasure to have such a man come to our church. As Mom stood in the foyer of the church, she saw a black couple enter via the front doors. I believe we had one black man in the church at that point so it seems like this would have been a non-issue. Sadly, it wasn't! Upon entering, the couple was greeted by an usher who promptly asked them to leave. However, there was an interesting twist to this situation. Not only did the black couple leave but also so did the evangelist! He left with them and took them to lunch! That was truly a sad thing to see. Thankfully, that evangelist had far more integrity and understanding of God's true nature than did the usher who asked the couple to leave. This was something that should have never happened, no matter what city or state or country we live.

To be completely honest, I never have and never will preach a "traditional" salvation message. Instead, I simply present the truth about God and His loving nature. The Bible is very clear concerning the fact that it is the goodness of God that leads man to repentance **(Romans 2:4 & Titus 2:11-12)**. When people hear that God loved us so much that He sent a sacrifice to stand in our place for all of our sins, they get excited and say, "Why wouldn't I want to be in relationship with such a loving God?" Nevertheless, when we present a God who is going to test a new believer and put them through difficult times to see what they are made of, many will run in the opposite direction. They get enough of that on the job. Many call it discipleship and believe that there is a short honeymoon period when a person first becomes born again. They believe the 'honeymoon' will end and then God will pour on the struggles to see how a person can handle himself or herself. There is so much that is wrong with that way of thinking.

Let's face it; we don't do this sort of thing to our loved ones. We want to walk them through everything and even have them learn by example as opposed to experience. In the Bible, Paul even admonishes us to learn this way:

1 Corinthians 10:6, Now these things were our examples, to the intent we should not lust after evil things, as they also lusted.

136

1 Corinthians 10:11, Now all these things happened unto them for examples: and they are written for our admonition, upon whom the ends of the world are come.

God wants His children to learn from the mistakes of others just as a loving parent does. God does not put problems in our lives to see what we are made of but has rather given us His Word to learn from **(2 Timothy 3:16)**. Therefore, we cannot say that God is the one who allows or causes problems in our lives. Let's not forget that Job did not have the advantage of having a Bible to read such as we have today. God's intention is to use His Word to show us how to live. Before we leave this particular topic, allow me to add one more bit of information.

You may be asking a question such as, "Doesn't the Bible say that God will test us?" The answer to this question is yes. However, we need to understand what a *"test"* from God truly is. I believe the Amplified Bible best offers some insight into this particular question.

1 Thessalonians 2:4, But just as we have been approved by God to be entrusted with the glad tidings (the Gospel), so we speak not to please men but to please God, Who tests our hearts [[a]expecting them to be approved]. (Amplified Translation)

The Bible does say God will test us but this does not come through any sort of experiences such as losing a job, a child, a spouse, or any other form of worldly difficulty or crises.

We need to understand that 1 Thessalonians is not meant to be used in the context in which some use it. God has entrusted us to preach the nearly-too-good-to-be-true news of the Gospel. It is the goodness of God that leads mankind to repentance **(Romans 2:4)**. God knows our motives better than we do. If God is testing us, it is not for His sake but rather for our own. This is done to reveal areas in our lives which we may need to adjust. In order to go out and tell others about the truth of the Gospel we must lay aside our own feelings and agendas. Many that are in the ministry struggle to do this. They don't want to offend anyone and run them off from their church or ministry since that may mean a loss of income. However, this also reveals a total lack of faith in God to be their provider.

According to **James 1:13**, we are not to say that we are tempted of God when it comes to evil. In researching the word "test", we will see that this word literally means, "to be tempted". If God does not tempt us with evil then we can say that He does not test us with anything that would tempt us to get angry at Him or at others. We can say that God will test us by tempting us to do good, such as preaching the Gospel. A test from God is not going to involve pain and suffering. However, it may involve having to put our pride aside to go and minister to that person out in public who looks like their having a bad day. If we pray for someone publicly, (outside of the church) we are sure to attract some attention. This is "a test", an opportunity to put our pride, reputation, status in the community, aside and allow God to flow through us.

In Job chapter 16, we see Job reproving his friends for a lack of mercy. I have already touched on the fact that some people mean well to begin with, but do not always comfort those who are in the midst of difficult times. I believe Job's friends at first meant well however when

Job did not respond the way they wanted him to, they began to focus on their own agendas and deal with Job out of pride, as opposed to dealing with him out of love. Let's not forget that they had also not received the same revelation that we have available today concerning God's true nature. Job even begins complaining about the cruelty of his three friends in chapter 19.

Job 19:23, Oh that my words were now written! oh that they were printed in a book!

Job got what he said in this case! His words were indeed written in a book for all to see. Nevertheless, I do wonder if Job regretted this. As you will see in a forthcoming chapter, Job came to regret the words he spoke of the Lord. Job also said he wanted his words to be written with an iron pen **(Job 19:24)**. He was serious about this!

One of the most interesting aspects of the Old Testament is the fact that there are so many prophecies pointing to the future. These are referred to as "types and shadows". We see one of these "types and shadows" in **Job 19:26** where Job said, "***And though after my skin worms destroy this body, yet in my flesh shall I*** *see God."* This is truly a powerful prophecy! The day will come for each of us when our bodies will return to dust. However, a day will also come when there will be a resurrection of our physical bodies. This was something Job could not have known about in the same manner as we do today.

Let's move ahead to Job chapter 23. We are about to see some real ignorance on Job's part but again, this is nothing we don't see today as well. I don't know about you but I have made the ignorant choice of trying to walk this same path and I can now admit to how wrong I was in doing so. It has been a long time since I did this, but the bottom line is that I have done what we are about to see Job do and so have many others.

Job 23:3, Oh that I knew where I might find him! that I might come even to his seat!

Wow! Job is showing some real arrogance as well as ignorance in this statement. He wants to see God face to face, but not for the purpose of bowing down to worship God. Instead, Job is longing for the opportunity to put his finger in God's face and tell Him a thing or two!

This is truly amazing but as I have already said, many of us have been guilty of doing the same thing. Job goes on to say that he wants to plead his case with God and proclaim that God has been unjust in all that He did to him **(Job 23:4)**. This is laying the foundation for what will ultimately aid us in understanding the book of Job.

Chapter 13

God Begins Speaking Through Elihu

—— W ——

By the time we reach Job chapter 27, Job has become extremely angry. His friends who supposedly came to his aid have done absolutely nothing to help. Job's lack of knowledge concerning God and His ways becomes more and more obvious. Some of us have lived-out actions similar to Job's. Of course, I am not saying this to condemn anyone. Nevertheless, these things need to be said. I myself have been guilty of these same things and have found that being offended can be the beginning of a very unhealthy path to walk.

Why, you may ask? It's quite simple! When we are offended, it simply shows that we need to make some changes in one or more areas of our life. We become offended when we are focused inwardly and not outwardly.

One person we have not heard about yet goes by the name of Elihu. He speaks out against Job and his three friends via the inspiration of the Holy Spirit. This is where we will begin to finally put things together concerning what truly took place and why it did. I know we have already looked at the fact that God is not the one who chooses what does and does not happen, but I think it will really sink in throughout the remainder of this study.

Job 32:1-3, "So these three men ceased to answer Job, because he was righteous in his own eyes. 2 Then was kindled the wrath of Elihu the son of Barachel the Buzite, of the kindred of Ram: against Job was his wrath kindled, because he justified himself rather than God. 3 Also against his three friends was his wrath kindled, because they had found no answer, and yet had condemned Job.

These three verses are essentially a summary of the entire book of Job. Job did not do anything directly to deserve what had happened to him. However, Job's three friends were incorrect to condemn him as the main cause of his problems. They tried to proclaim that Job's own sin had brought on the terrible events but could never be specific to exactly what that sin was. This was because they truly did not know what they were talking about. Job also went from a state of simply being selfish, to one of pure ignorance as he moved to condemn God over what had taken place; even going as far as to call God unjust.

One of the most interesting things about Elihu is the fact that he had sat idly by and listened to what was being said between Job and his three friends for some time. He didn't just interrupt everything that took place and speak out of turn. He was wise to wait until the time was right before he spoke. I consider this a great quality that we should all exemplify. We see this taking shape in **Job 32:4-5** as Elihu waited to speak until he saw that there was no answer in the mouths of Job's three friends.

Elihu was very straightforward and none too shy in what he had to say. He chose both his words and timing with respect for those he was speaking to. Nevertheless, he did not hold back in speaking what he believed to be the truth to these four men. I believe there is a way to be up-front and honest and still get our point across. I also believe that a person, who can be offended, probably should be offended. If they are mature, their offense should make them take a step back and ask what it is that causes them to be offended. The offence should establish a need for changing the way they are thinking or believing. Their actions or reactions may need to be redirected. If they are immature, they are going to be offended no matter what is said to them.

I truly believe that we should also study out **Job 32:6-9** in order to see the proper way to deal with relationships. Acting out of impatience normally results in anger and that of course will cause others to become angry. There is never any sort of resolution when that type of thing takes place. Respect for one another is very important. We may not always agree at a particular moment, but that does not mean we have to become angry at one another and ruin friendships. The Bible is very clear about living at peace with one another as much as it is possible **(Romans 12:18)**.

Elihu goes on to say that he is going to give his opinion, but he also says that he was stirred up by the Lord. This is a very important point in understanding the book of Job. What God was about to speak through Elihu will help us to see that God was truly not the reason for Job's problems nor did He simply choose to allow Satan to instigate those problems.

Elihu is a prime example of the fact that wisdom is not always determined by age. When we allow God to speak through us, age makes no difference. He will always make us look really good! We may even appear to be much smarter than we really are!

Job 32:6, "And Elihu the son of Barachel the Buzite answered and said, I am young, and ye are very old; wherefore I was afraid, and durst not shew you mine opinion."

Elihu was bold but not arrogant. He understood his place and was willing to submit to his elders. Nevertheless, when his elders were unable to understand what was taking place concerning Job, he stepped in to shed light on the situation. He was quick to hear and slow to speak, as we are all instructed to be according to **James 1:19**. I have already stated that we can learn a lot from the book of Job, and this particular instance is no exception. In this modern day and age, most young people have little to no respect for their elders. However, respect for our elders is a Biblical and necessary quality, but that does not mean we should just sit back and never speak up at the right time. Elihu did so boldly, but he also did so with respect. If he can do it so can we!

He waited for his elders to speak truth concerning the matter they were involved in, but when they never did, he realized it was time to step up and speak himself. Let's not forget that Elihu was being inspired of God to speak up. He did not simply do this because he wanted to from his own fleshly understanding.

You may be wondering when Elihu came on the scene. According to what we see in scripture, he was actually present the entire time but was patient and did not speak out of turn. In **Job 32:11** he says *"Behold, I waited for your words; I gave ear to your reasons, whilst ye searched out what to say."*

What Job's three friends had spoken to him was obviously incorrect. We will see God say the same thing in a later chapter. These three friends had placed the full blame for the evil that Job had experienced on God and proclaimed that it came due to great sin in Job's life. This of course was not true as we have already seen. Nevertheless, keep in mind that there was no Bible available for Job or his three friends to read during their lifetimes. They did not have the available knowledge that you and I have today.

Job and his three friends had been involved in a lot of arguing. Nevertheless, when Elihu began to speak under the anointing of God, it was so strong that all of the arguing instantly ceased. We see this in *Job 32:15-17*.

Job 32:21-22 "I won't play favorites or try to flatter anyone. 22 For if I tried flattery, my Creator would soon destroy me."

Elihu is simply issuing a statement concerning what he is about to share. He wants everyone present to understand that he is not doing so to win any man's favor. In other words, he is not going to speak due to any reason that puts the focus on him. This was not about himself but about ministering to those around him. Let's face it, Job and his three friends desperately needed to know the truth. In many cases, ministering to others may involve a rebuke. This was the case with Elihu and Job as well as Job's three friends. He was not going to tell Job and his three friends what they wanted to hear, but rather what they needed to hear.

God was speaking through Elihu via the Holy Spirit for the purpose of not showing His anger first hand to Job and his friends. By this time in the book of Job, God *was* angry after the way Job and his friends had been acting toward Him. (Remember, this is happening even prior to the Old Covenant) What Elihu was saying was due to divine inspiration from God **(Job 33:4)**.

Elihu was in complete support of a response from Job concerning what he had to say to him. However, as it turned out, Job did not have time to respond due to the fact that God spoke up and intervened by speaking to Job directly.

Job 33:7, "So you don't need to be afraid of me. I won't come down hard on you."

This is referring back to a statement made by Job to his three friends in **Job 13:21** when he said, **"Withdraw thine hand far from me: and let not thy dread make me afraid."** Job had made this statement concerning the Lord because he believed it was God who had been the root cause of his problems.

Job was still working to make claims that his problems had not come from great sin in his life.

He was correct in saying this. Remember, God is not going to send problems into our lives in order to punish us. That would negate the purpose of Jesus hanging on the cross. However, Job was no different from any other human, with the exception of Jesus, who ever walked on the Earth. His sins did not bring his problems upon him but that did not make him a non-sinner. Job was proclaiming that he deserved better than what he was experiencing and based this upon his own merit and ability. Job continued to blame God for what had happened and asserted his own integrity above God's! That is purely wrong, yet not uncommon, even today. This is what we are saying when we believe that we need to read our Bible, pray and go to church each time the doors are open in order for God to bless us. We are relying on our own abilities. We have probably all been in this same boat at some point or another. I can bear witness to the fact that it creates much frustration.

No matter how well we live, none of us deserves the mercy and grace given freely from God. Job believed he deserved better and believed this should come based on his own performance. God gave mercy concerning Job's arrogance and did not give him what he deserved. If God had imputed Job's sins unto him, Job would have welcomed the troubles he experienced over God's wrath. There is a great lesson for us to learn from Job's experiences.

Job did the right thing when he rejected the notion of his friends, when they said his problems came because of great sin in his life. Nevertheless, Job was just as wrong as we are when he tried to tie God's blessings in his life to his individual performance. Remember, we did not go from being a sinner to a born again Christian based upon our individual works. In the same manner, we are to continue to trust God with that same kind of faith that it took to become born again in the first place **(Colossians 2:6)**.

We need to remember that God is not obligated to explain Himself. I have already given explanations to the affect that Job's problems were not from or of God, but Job did not see things that way. If he had been right in blaming God for what took place, God would have never been obligated to give an explanation as to why things took place as they did. Don't forget, we have established what I believe is the reason for Job's troubles, and that is the fact that Satan had control over the Earth and simply wanted to get back at God. He saw an opportunity with Job for many reasons, but I believe one of the primary reasons was due to Job's success.

If I were a general, fighting in a war, I would go after the biggest and the best target if I knew I had the ability to defeat them. Satan simply went after Job because he represented the biggest target.

Job 33:24, "Then he is gracious unto him, and saith, Deliver him from going down to the pit: I have found a ransom."

This is a key scripture in understanding the book of Job. It is not uncommon, for God to be misrepresented in the modern church. It is said that He is angry and is basing His love for us on our own individual performance. If we believe that way, we are just as wrong as Job was and need someone like Elihu to come along and tell us the truth. That is exactly what Elihu was doing in **Job 33:24**. He was telling Job that God was the complete opposite of what he had believed. God is eager to show His mercy and grace toward mankind, but it is most certainly not what Job had believed. **(Job 33:11)**.

Elihu is not willing to condemn God **(Job 33:32)**. We need to learn to follow this model as well! There may be people around us who want to point the finger at God when bad things happen, just like Eliphaz, Bildad, Zophar and even Job, but we need to listen to the Elihu's in our lives instead.

Chapter 14

The Truth Begins to Unravel

We have seen a lot take place up to this point. By simply reading the book of Job alone, it would be very easy to believe that God was the reason for Job's troubles. However, we have also traveled outside the book of Job to provide an accurate Biblical explanation as to why Job experienced the bad situations that trampled all over his life. I truly believe many people do not make it to the end of Job, which means they do not see what ultimately takes place between God, Job, and his three friends.

Do you remember **1 Corinthians 10:6 & 11**? We are admonished to learn by example and not by experience. There are many situations in the Bible that we do not want to see repeated in our own lives. So many people will take anything at all and say, "It's in the Bible" That is as if to say we should take anything we see in the Bible and believe that we can apply it directly to our own personal experiences. This is how the book of

Job is commonly used by the majority. However, that does not mean we should follow the majority **(Matthew 7:13-14)**.

Let's say for example, we have betrayed a friend in some form or fashion. Does this mean we *should* compare ourselves to Judas Iscariot, just as many compare themselves to Job? I sincerely hope not, because we also see in scripture where Judas hung himself **(Matthew 27:5)**. So, does that mean we should also hang ourselves? The answer is simply, NO*!* Just as we should not go to the extreme of hanging ourselves, we should never compare ourselves to Job or seek to identify with anything spoken by Eliphaz, Bildad, or Zophar.

Job 34:5, "For Job hath said, I am righteous: and God hath taken away my judgment."

This verse sums up Job's position. He was accurate to proclaim that he was living a righteous life and his problems did not come as a result of any individual sin in his life. Nevertheless, he was still wrong to look to God as the source of his problems. The obvious choice, was to look to God as the sole power in the universe, and as such, being the only logical explanation for such a catastrophe. This is what many denominations of the church still do today. They believe that God is using our problems to make us strong or to bring glory to Himself in some way. They have taken Satan out of the equation all together. Remember **James 4:7**? "We" are to resist the Devil. God does not work through the Devil but we need to remember that his chief purpose is to thwart any and every good thing in our lives. If we fail to resist him, it is we who are allowing Satan to successfully attack us.

Elihu continues in **Job 34:6** by reminding Job of some of the things he had spoken in his own defense. Job had proclaimed that it was God who had afflicted him unjustly.

Elihu tells Job that it was wrong to side with the ungodly **(Job 34:8-9)** and say that God does not bless and take care of the righteous. Job was also wrong to proclaim that there is no advantage to living a righteous life. Just as is the case with so many other events we have studied from Job, this is a common idea believed in the modern day church.

God was not in the wrong by not stepping in and keeping Satan from attacking Job. As we have already established, God governs Himself by laws and does not come back and re-write those laws when it is convenient. He had given man control over the Earth and in turn, man gave that control over to Satan. God obviously had the 'power' to keep Satan from attacking Job but due to the fact that God always keeps His Word **(Hebrews 1:3)**, He could not stop Satan from doing what he did without violating that Word.

Job 34:13, "Who put [God] in charge over the Earth? Or who laid on Him the whole world?" (Amplified Translation)

What an amazing statement! This adds a lot of strength to the foundational reason as to why I wrote this book. Elihu is essentially saying, "Who put God in control of the Earth?"

It is really easy to assume that God created the Earth, so He must be the one who controls what takes place on the Earth. We have already looked at the Sovereignty of God in some detail and established the fact that God put man in control of the Earth. Yes, there are still some things that God retains control of such as time, when the sun rises and sets, the rotation of every planet, our solar system and so on. However,

He does not choose or control what does and does not happen in our individual lives.

Job 34:32, "Or 'I don't know what evil I have done—tell me. If I have done wrong, I will stop at once'?" (New Living Translation)

We can learn a lot from this verse. Job did not need to confess something that he did not do. There was truly no individual sin in Job's life that led to his problems. This is a common scenario played out today as well. If Job had not simply assumed that he knew what was going on, he could have taken the time to ask God to show him. God would have spoken to Job concerning what he did not understand just as He is willing to do with us when we don't understand. God loves us and is not interested in leaving us in the dark!

Job 34:35, "Job speaks out of ignorance; his words lack insight." (New Living Translation)

This summary should help clear up a lot of misunderstanding in a few simple words. *Job did not know what he was talking about and neither did his three friends.* Elihu was the only one who had spoken any true wisdom up to this point.

Job 34:36, "My desire is that Job may be tried unto the end because of his answers for wicked men."

Elihu was speaking based on the fact that he realized Job had received inaccurate counsel from his three friends. Yet Elihu agreed with God, go figure, that Job was completely wrong to blame God for what had taken place. He also knew that Job's friends had done nothing to help the situation. They had simply come in and strengthened Job's wrong views with their own.

Job was truly wrong to side with his three friends and ultimately say there was no advantage to living as a righteous man.

Have you ever been wrongfully accused of something you did not do? If you have then you know how difficult it can be. God is accused of doing so many terrible things, yet He does not ever give any of us what we deserve. God finally reached a point in which He spoke up on His own behalf beginning in Job chapter 38.

Job 38:2, "Who is this that questions my wisdom with such ignorant words?" (New Living Translation)

God had reached the breaking point! He was unpleased with the fact that He was being falsely accused for something He did not cause or even allow. In turn, God demanded an answer from Job concerning this matter. **Job 38:2** proves the fact that Job did not know what he was talking about when he said *"The Lord gave and the Lord has taken away"*, in **Job 1:21.** Job spoke based on a tremendous lack of knowledge. He had allowed the unwise counsel of his friends to strengthen further his wrong perspective of the situation. They were blinded, just as many are today. I am not saying this to put anybody down but rather to make a very important point.

God truly is amazing! I don't mind if a person says, *"God is in control"* when it applies to the fact that He is all-powerful. God is so powerful to the point that He can use His own creation to show a person when they are in the wrong, and this is exactly what He did with Job. If you would like to read about this, refer to **Job 38:4-11**.

God wanted to know who Job thought he was to accuse Him of such terrible things. Job had made a common mistake that most, if not all of us have made at one point or another. He made an assumption based on a lack of knowledge. The bottom line is that there is always lack when we assume.

As I already mentioned, there are still some things that God retains full control over such as the seasons, and when the sun rises and sets. Most importantly, He unchangingly retains control over His own integrity no matter what. However, there are so many other aspects where God has put mankind in control. Let's look at the weather as an example:

Our ministry, (Winlight Ministries) was holding a large event in Louisiana. The event was scheduled to take place on a Friday and Saturday. The weather forecast did not look good as the chance for major storms went up more and more with each day leading up to the event. I, along with others associated with our ministry, began to tell the weather that it must be calm and clear. The forecast continued to call for major storms and the potential for tornadoes. I refused to just sit back and say, "God is in control. If He wants the storms to come, they will". Instead, I looked to **Mark 11:23-24** and simply spoke to the weather system and told it to go around us. The weather was great Friday night and the sun was out all day on Saturday! We did not receive a single drop of rain during the event. If I had assumed that God was in full control of the weather, we would have more than likely, had a smaller turnout during the event due to bad weather. You may not agree with this line of thinking but I have no reason to change because it is working out in a positive way for me. It can work the same way for you as well!

God continued His dialog with Job by asking him questions, to show him how ignorant he really was sounding. How could Job know why the Earth simply hangs, suspended in the middle of the universe? God was simply asking Job where he was when He created the universe. God was "laying it on thick" at this point. If Job was sitting down, I am sure he was sinking lower and lower into his seat! God hit Job with a lot of information in the remainder of chapter 38. There is no doubt that Job was beginning to see how wrong he truly had been. When we blame God, we need to see the error of our ways in the same manner. Who are we to believe that

God is guilty? Let's not forget about that enemy of ours who has come *only* to steal, kill, and destroy **(John 10:10)**. Moreover, just in case you need a reminder, God does not control what the Devil can and cannot do (James 4:7).

The Lord goes on to give Job an open door, to declare the inner most workings of the Earth, the heavens, and man's heart.

Job 39:1, "Do you know when the wild goats give birth? Have you watched as deer are born in the wild?" (New Living Translation)

God wanted Job to see how little knowledge he really had. I believe Job was getting the picture by this point. Job's prideful attitude was beginning to wash away. Nevertheless, God doesn't stop with **Job 39:1**. He continues to use His creation in a powerful effort to drive His point home to Job. God easily showed Job how powerless he was as a man. Job's tail was between his legs by the time this was all said and done.

Chapter 15

Job Humbles Himself

We have covered a lot of material to this point. Now we are going to put it all together, enabling us to understand why we should *not* blame God when bad things happen. Unfortunately, there are many of us who have stood on the book of Job to say that God allows the Devil to do bad things. Many have also used this book to form other wrong doctrines that are just as destructive, like believing that God will bring tragedy into our lives as a form of judgment for our own personal sins. I believe I have sufficiently countered much of the wrong doctrine based on the book of Job. Nevertheless, I encourage you to study the Word of God for yourself, and allow God to reveal to you the truth about what I have taught.

God had begun dealing with Job in a very *direct* manner starting with chapter 38 and we will soon see the result of God's questioning, as

Job responds in a different manner and attitude than what we have heard from him up to this point.

Job knew that sin was not the issue in the tragedies he had been dealt. He had not allowed what his friends were speaking to him, to cause any misunderstanding. However, Job was not entirely in the right in his actions. He believed that God was unjust and had not treated him fairly. We know he sinned **(Romans 8:23)** but this was not a specific sin that caused the great disasters that came upon him; however he had sinned since then, by falsely accusing God of being the source of his troubles.

In **Job 40:3-4**, we see Job's response to God. He begins to repent as he admits his need to shut his mouth and refrain from further wrong speaking as God continues to rebuke Job over the course of the next few verses. We then see these words spoken by God in **Job 40:8**, *"Wilt thou also disannul my judgment? wilt thou condemn me, that thou mayest be righteous?"*

Job blamed and condemned God for what had taken place in his life. He had done so in a very arrogant manner as if to say, he was simply too righteous to have dealt with such terrible circumstances. Job did what many of us have done. He arrived at an inaccurate conclusion, which was to say that he did nothing to deserve such difficulties. In turn, he believed that God had dealt with him in an unjust manner. Of course, we know that it was Satan who was to blame for what had taken place. In a roundabout way, mankind was ultimately responsible as he was the one who allowed sin to enter into the world in the first place, *not* God. This of course, allowed Satan to have control of the Earth.

Job 40:12, "Look on every one that is proud, and bring him low; and tread down the wicked in their place." (New Living Translation)

God was in the process of humbling Job who was in need of a lot of salt, to aid in swallowing his large amount of pride. I believe we can learn quite a bit from **Job 40:12**. In simplest terminology, God was disciplining Job. However, God was doing this not via pain or suffering but rather through His Word. This is the way as scripture says, that He disciplines His children.

2 Timothy 3:16, "All scripture is given by inspiration of God, and is profitable for doctrine, for reproof, for correction, for instruction in righteousness."

God does *not* discipline us with pain and suffering as Job's friends claimed. Many in the church today still believe that God will do bad things to us as a result of sin in our lives. Believing in such a manner as this, throws Jesus right under the bus, so-to-speak. However, **2 Timothy 3:16** makes it very clear that God disciplines us through His Word. Job may not have had the written Word of God as we do today, but God dealt with him in the same manner as He does with us.

God eventually gave Job an opportunity to show his own power and ability, and of course, Job could *not* deliver **(Job 40:14)**. Job needed to be brought down from the pedestal on which he had placed himself.

Early on in this book, I mentioned the fact that I would not dissect the book of Job one verse at a time. While I have covered a lot of material, I have also left much out. I want to continue to encourage you to research on your own and allow God to give you your own revelation.

As we reach the final chapter of chapter 42, we see a man finally surrendering in humility and submitting himself to the Lord.

Job 42:1-6, "Then Job replied to the LORD: 2 I know that you can do anything, and no one can stop you. 3 You asked, 'Who is this that questions my wisdom with such ignorance? It is I—and I was talking about things I knew nothing about, things far too wonderful for me. 4 You said, 'Listen and I will speak! I have some questions for you, and you must answer them. 5 I had only heard about you before, but now I have seen you with my own eyes. 6 I take back everything I said, and I sit in dust and ashes to show my repentance." (New Living Translation)

Job had allowed his emotions to get in the way of what he truly knew. Deep down, Job knew that he was wrong to go on such a tirade against God. He reacted in the shear heat of the moment. This is similar to what happened to Peter when he took his eyes off Jesus in **Matthew 14:30-31**. Peter began to sink and was full of fear. If he had kept his focus on Jesus, fear, which is an emotion of selfishness, would have never entered the picture, or at the least, it would not have dominated the scene.

Job ultimately repents and turns from his selfishness and wrong thinking in verses 1-6 of the last chapter. These final verses make it clear that Job came to the understanding that God was *not* the one to blame for his troubles. He admits that he does not know what really took place; nevertheless, it was *not* God who was to blame.

So what ever happened to Job's three friends: Eliphaz, Bildad, and Zophar? In an earlier chapter, I said that Eliphaz was the leader of this group of three, as he spoke more than any of the others. I believe this point is solidified in the next verse by God, Himself.

Job 42:7, "After the LORD had finished speaking to Job, he said to Eliphaz the Temanite: "I am angry with you and your two friends, for you have not spoken accurately about me, as my servant Job has." (New Living Translation)

I have been looking forward to writing about **Job 42:7** since chapter one of this book! The majority of Christians cite the book of Job during disastrous times, saying that God allows bad things to happen for a multitude of reasons. Many will also cite what Job's friends had to say. They follow the line of thinking that says God will do terrible things to us in order to punish us for great sin in our lives, then bless us when we have come through our difficulties. **Job 42:7** dispels all of that nonsense!

God literally and clearly states, *"I am not the one to blame for what happened to Job!"* We can also conclude that God is not to blame when bad things happen to us. Job's friends had not spoken of what is true about God! This is amazing! It was truly not sin that brought on Job's problems. We can now firmly dismiss this area of wrong thinking. Even though Job's friends followed a common way of thinking still used in the church today, God clearly told them how wrong they were to say that He was judging Job, among other things. This was even pre-Jesus, and therefore we have even more reason to believe that God is not doing bad things to us due to sin, or for any other reason.

So, what was the punishment for Eliphaz, Bildad, and Zophar? In order for these three men to appease God's anger towards them, a sacrifice offering had to be made. This is another type and shadow, that points directly to Jesus hanging on the cross. Even though the three friends were guilty, they were able to atone for their sins with a sacrifice that stood in the gap for them, just as Jesus later did for all mankind.

In **Job 42:8-9,** God also instructed Job to pray for his three friends as part of their repentance. After all of their efforts to proclaim how right they were, in saying it was God who hit Job with such great problems due to sin in his life, they had to humble themselves. They now had to submit themselves to Job, which took true humility, exactly what Eliphaz, Bildad, and Zophar needed. I also believe this same concept needs to take place often, in the modern day church, as so many people tend to place themselves above others. I have even heard many ministers cite their credentials to say they are better than the layperson. This is as wrong as the notions of Job's friends.

It is also very interesting to see that God did not require the same repentance from Job that He did of his three friends. I believe this may be similar to what took place with David in the book of Psalms. David could have offered sacrifices, but God truly wanted David to repent and turn from his evil ways. If we repent, we are turning in the opposite direction. This takes the renewal of our minds and it will be long lasting as opposed to a temporary sacrifice. Don't forget, there has only been one sacrifice that will last forever and that is the sacrifice of Jesus.

Job 42:10, "And the LORD turned the captivity of Job, when he prayed for his friends: also the LORD gave Job twice as much as he had before."

God did not take anything from Job in order to give it back to him later. That simply is not the true nature of God. Job had become focused on himself through all of his trouble, but after the discipline of the Lord, he repented. This opened the door for God to be able to bless Job with twice as much as he had before. Job's actions brought on the blessing, but he had to listen and respond to God before the door to such a blessing could open. What the enemy meant for evil, God used for Job's good, and God will *always* do so for His children*!*

WINLIGHT MINISTRIES
www.wlmi.org

Notes

Notes

Notes

Notes

Notes

Made in the USA
Lexington, KY
13 March 2011